A House Divided

THE STORY OF IKE AND MCCARTHY

A House Divided

Donald J. Farinacci

NAVIGATOR BOOKS

SAN DIEGO, CALIFORNIA

A HOUSE DIVIDED

Copyright © 2015 by Donald J. Farinacci

Navigator Books

www.navigator-books.com

ISBN-13: 978-1-940397-52-8

Printed in the United States of America

"...A political party divided against itself, half McCarthy and half Eisenhower, could not produce national unity...."

—Adlai Stevenson

"...If we allow ourselves to be persuaded that every individual, or party, that takes issue with our own convictions is necessarily wicked or treasonous – then we are approaching the end of freedom's road."

—Dwight David Eisenhower

"The fate of the world rests with the clash between the atheism of Moscow and the Christian spirit throughout other parts of the world."

—Joseph R. McCarthy

FOREWORD

What follows is a story of both great political and personal drama. From February of 1950 to June of 1954, the conscience of America was hijacked – not by a person but rather by a political movement known as "McCarthyism". During that four and a half year period, McCarthyism cost countless Americans their jobs, their careers, their reputations, their friends and their futures.

Having as its raison d'etre the elimination of Communists and Communist sympathizers from public life, the movement was not without legitimate – even worthy - roots. America of the late 1940's and early 50's was permeated by fear and anxiety over a real threat to its national security. In the abstract, the threat came from the insidious brand of international communism which endangered both nations and populations from the outside; and subverted them from within.

In more concrete terms, the brand of aggressive communism practiced by the mega-nations, the Soviet Union and Red China, seemed to be winning the Cold War, as they gobbled up smaller countries and exercised hegemony over their lands and populations. From the Communist threat of overtly attacking, conquering the most vulnerable countries; and undermining others through espionage and internal subversion, the perception held by many was that the Communist super-powers were moving inexorably towards world domination.

In their arsenal were huge armies in strategically advantageous positions gained during World War II; and acquired by them most recently were nuclear weapons. Without question, the America of the World War II era had planted the seeds of McCarthyism by its excessively benign view of the Soviet Union, its ally in the war against Nazi Germany and Imperial Japan.

The unintended consequence of the national myopia of pre-war and wartime America about international communism, was the spawning of a political force – McCarthyism – which by 1952 had become a real and present danger to the fundamental civil liberties contained in the Bill of

Rights. These included freedom of speech, freedom of assembly, freedom of the press and the right not to be deprived of liberty or property without due process of law.

But, though McCarthyism's originator and chief spokesman, Senator Joseph R. McCarthy of Wisconsin, gained tremendous popularity and power in the early 50's, there did exist desultory opposition to his methods. Certain prominent Americans such as Senator Margaret Chase Smith of Maine, Journalist Edward R. Murrow, Governor Thomas E. Dewey of New York and Presidents Truman and Eisenhower mounted consistent though non-unified resistance and countermeasures to what they viewed as McCarthy's undermining of the United States Constitution and the Rule of Law.

The least visible but no less dramatic and historically significant opposition was mounted over a two and a half year period by candidate and then President, Dwight D. Eisenhower. His battle with McCarthy and McCarthyism was little noticed and little known. In the end, however, it proved decisive. This is the story of that mostly invisible struggle.

Very few chronicles of the detailed campaign by President Eisenhower against Joe McCarthy and his methods exist; but I hope by this history to add to a better understanding of the full story and its impact upon America.

The story has gone largely untold, and I have attempted here to give it a more prominent place. It is an integral part of the history of the Cold War, without which such history is incomplete.

It is not a dry historical narrative. It is a vital retrospective filled with human drama, passion, cowardice and courage. It is also not a tome, a thesis or a polemic – but merely a story – one which I have researched and sought to substantiate in every important respect. I have referred to it as "a history" and my method has been that of an historian, not a polemicist.

Donald Farinacci

March, 2014

CONTENTS

PART I – THE ROAD TO FAME

PART II – MCCARTHY AND THE ARMY

PART III – THE FALL

"I do not like the way the Senate has been made a rendezvous for vilification for selfish political gain at the sacrifice of individual reputations and national unity."

—Senator Margaret Chase Smith
Speaking on McCarthyism,
June 1, 1950

"...I'm not going to compromise my ideals and personal beliefs for a few stinking votes. To hell with it."

—Dwight D. Eisenhower,
March, 1954.

CHAPTER ONE

Genesis of an Estrangement — 1952

The autumn of 1952 should have been a time of undiluted personal satisfaction for Dwight David Eisenhower, the Republican nominee for President of the United States. Yet the nation's top military hero — though upbeat and positive for the most part — had found a troubling ambivalence leeching into his channels of thought.

His long-time nickname, "Ike," had been embraced and enthusiastically adopted by an admiring fan-base of over a hundred million people. Nevertheless, Eisenhower found himself on the twin horns of a dilemma, from which no amount of crowd adulation could extricate him. In the midst of an ocean of placards, which read, "I Like Ike" and "Let Adlai go the other way," he was stuck in a conundrum.

As the Republican candidate for President, but a relative newcomer to politics, Eisenhower needed the support of the leaders of his party, including its biggest star, Senator Joseph R. McCarthy of Wisconsin. Yet, at the same time he loathed the "ism" attached to McCarthy's name. Truth be told, he didn't care much for Joe McCarthy either, considering him a demagogue and a fraud; and to Ike, "McCarthyism" was anathema.

Joseph McCarthy, with his deep voice, nervous laugh and enigmatic smile, had been awarded the sobriquet, "Tail gunner Joe" by his supporters, allegedly in recognition of acts of valor during air combat in World War II — an appellation at best exaggerated and at worst invented.

But no matter, by 1952, Joe McCarthy had been building up a head of steam since arriving in Washington in 1947 to assume a seat in the United States Senate. This was a good five years before Eisenhower had even decided he himself was a Republican — much less a petitioner to be named his party's standard bearer.

McCarthy had flirted with several political causes as a new senator before finally settling in 1949 on militant anti-communism exclusively — one which seemed to stick with the American public and offered the greatest potential for garnering vast amounts of publicity. Chiefly instrumental in persuading McCarthy to adopt anti-communism as his raison d'etre was his friend and fellow Roman Catholic, Edmund Walsh, himself a militant anti-communist.

Strident anti-communism would be McCarthy's path to fame, albeit one which eventually morphed into notoriety.

McCarthy's quest for public attention was built upon verbal assaults on his chosen targets, usually not stopping short of character assassination. His methods were beautiful in their simplicity: Under the shield of congressional immunity, he would call a public figure a "communist", a "pinko", a "fellow traveler" or a "communist sympathizer" ("comsymp"); and let it be repeated over and over by the media and other McCarthyites until it took hold in the minds of the public — and all without having to offer a shred of evidence to support his accusation. It was the stuff which made Machiavelli's "The Prince" a timeless classic.

Ad hominem attacks worked. And to McCarthy the truth or falsity of the charges was immaterial. What counted was their publicity-potential. The more sensational the accusation, the bigger the public-attention dividend it paid. His attacks were crudely designed to feed upon the fear Americans felt because of a nuclear-armed Soviet Union combined with internal subversion in the United States: "I have here in my hand a list of 205...a list of names (of Communists in the State Department) still working, and shaping the policy of the State Department (Joseph R. McCarthy, Wheeling, W. Virginia, February 9, 1950). By the following day the number of Communists on McCarthy's list had dwindled to 57, although no overnight mass exodus of Communists from either the State Department or the Communist Party had been noticed. As he continued his campaign trip, the number expanded to 207 "bad risks" and contracted to 81 "loyalty risks".

The argument that Joe McCarthy was simply a soldier in the Cold War has often been made. But fidelity to history requires that a major distinction be drawn. The Cold War targeted for the most part our foreign enemies. McCarthy's campaign was directed almost exclusively against other Americans — those who he considered the "enemy within".

No widespread campaign such as McCarthy's from 1950 through 1954 could have succeeded, however, without containing a basis in truth. McCarthy's offensive was no exception. There was internal subversion in the U.S. before and during the period in which McCarthy's star shone the brightest. Soviet spies had infiltrated at least the State, Treasury and Agriculture Departments. And internal espionage may have cost the United States its atomic secrets. Klaus Fuchs, Harry Gold, Julius and Ethel Rosenberg and Alger Hiss were among the best known American citizens or residents engaged as spies for the Soviet Union.

The problem with McCarthy was not that there weren't legitimate targets to pursue, but rather that he preferred the quick splash, the sensational allegation based on either the flimsiest of proof or no proof at all — accusations he skillfully exploited while whipping the public up into a frenzy.

The movement McCarthy spawned had been favored by the media of the early 1950's with the catch-phrase, "McCarthyism". And ingrained in McCarthyism was an innate — almost Darwinian — protective armor. His accusations were usually paper-thin or outright fabrications. Yet despite their flimsiness, they were mostly bullet-proof.

In a "Catch-22" twist, anyone was free to try to expose McCarthy as a fraud and his most outlandish accusations as lies or huge exaggerations, but if one did so, that fact alone was characterized by

McCarthyites as an act of "un-Americanism". McCarthy single-handedly changed the rules by which Americans played. Innuendo, insinuation, half-truths and defamation of character became acceptable, while free speech was largely circumscribed by what McCarthy, his associates and his disciples deemed acceptable. He redefined and reoriented the national discourse and its concept of liberty.

Hence, for a period of approximately five years in the late 40's and early 50's, Joseph McCarthy and his minions lied about people, ruined their reputations, cost them their jobs, destroyed their careers and exposed them to criminal investigation — all with impunity.

McCarthyism's protective armor held it in good stead. By 1952, Joe McCarthy was the most popular and powerful political figure in America.

None of this is to suggest that there was no merit at all to any of McCarthy's accusations. But considering the vast number of charges he leveled against public officials and private citizens alike, the number of criminal prosecutions resulting from his claims was almost non-existent. The most notorious spies prosecuted during the McCarthy era were exposed by others.

Contrariwise, the reputations and careers of innocent people destroyed by McCarthy were legion.

By late 1951 when Dwight D. Eisenhower finally yielded to his many supporters' pleas to resign as Commander-in-Chief of NATO and run for president on the Republican ticket, McCarthy was the force to be reckoned with — not only in the Republican Party but in all of American politics.

While some moderate Republicans, such as Eisenhower, Henry Cabot Lodge and Thomas E. Dewey, abhorred McCarthy's methods, they were at least initially afraid to speak out, lest they themselves be branded as communist sympathizers or worse.

To a certain extent Eisenhower could — and did — lay claim to ignorance of the dramatic escalation of McCarthy's smear campaigns and burgeoning fame in 1951 and well into 1952. During that time period Eisenhower was out of the Country, serving as Commanding General of NATO in Brussels, Belgium. But

Eisenhower was always better informed than he was willing to admit and far more intelligent than generally credited.

Behind his spectacular smile and surface affability there lay a shrewd and calculating intellect, one as easily given to deceit as to candor. Even while in Brussels, Eisenhower was kept apprised of what was going on with McCarthy back in Washington, D.C. and in the nation at large. His main sources of information were the members of the small but influential group of high-level advisers who were busy organizing grass-roots "Eisenhower for President" committees. Numbered among these supporters were the general's brother, Milton Eisenhower, Henry Cabot Lodge of Massachusetts, Tex McCrary of Texas and Sherman Adams, the former governor of New Hampshire.

Eisenhower silently deplored McCarthy's tactics. The Five-Star General could be very forceful when the situation called for it, but his style of leadership was based mainly on consensus — building and mediation — seeking common ground among adverse parties through conciliation and good will. He had used this methodology with extraordinary success in unifying the "Allies" during World War Two, to achieve victory over Nazi Germany. It was more in keeping with his personality, and indeed was the main reason Army Chief of Staff, General George C. Marshall, had selected Eisenhower in 1943 over men with more seniority and experience, to be Commander-In-Chief of all Allied Forces in Europe.

The legendary success which Eisenhower achieved in juggling the outsized egos of giants like Winston Churchill, Charles de Gaulle, General George S. Patton and Field Marshall Bernard Montgomery was a clear testament to his exceptional skills.

But, in the late summer of 1952, Eisenhower, who had just secured his party's nomination for president, found himself on a brand new playing field — one whose terrain was foreign to him — national politics — and whose rules he accepted only reluctantly and without relish.

On the other hand, Joe McCarthy had been practicing his brand of red-baiting for more than three years by the summer of 1952 with phenomenal success. He sat astride the top of the political pyramid in America, with no real competition. He was the "King of the Hill" and more than willing to knock anyone off who threatened his position at the top. He made no exception for the presidential standard bearer of his own party.

It was into this national climate of recrimination, fear and distrust that Ike had tossed his political hat.

Eisenhower's ascent to the pinnacle of the Republican Party had been very different than McCarthy's, but impressive nonetheless. In January of 1952, he still held his NATO post in Europe and had no intention of resigning to campaign. He firmly withstood the pressure to actively campaign, from supporters such as Cabot Lodge and McCrary, but did give them his approval to form "Eisenhower For President" committees. Hence the slogan, "I like Ike," was born.

Without ever setting foot on U.S. soil, Eisenhower won the New Hampshire Primary, established a formidable political machine in Texas; and finally returned home in the summer of 1952, a national hero, to proudly accept the Republican Party's nomination to be the nation's next president. But there was a dark underside to the nomination that portended trouble on the horizon.

Much of America was still in thrall to Joe McCarthy. And in the early stages of Eisenhower's campaign against Adlai Stevenson, the Democratic Party's nominee for president, an event occurred which would test the mettle of Dwight Eisenhower and shake his faith in his country, his party and himself.

CHAPTER TWO

Assault on an Icon

In July, 1947, President Harry S. Truman dispatched Lieutenant-General Albert C. Wedemeyer to China and Korea to trouble-shoot the unstable political, economic and military situations in those countries. Wedemeyer was an admirer of Generalissimo Chiang Kai-shek, Nationalist leader and dictator of China. The resulting "Wedemeyer Report" called for U.S. training and assistance to the nationalist armies embroiled in a civil war with communist forces led by Mao Tse Tung. Truman rejected Wedemeyer's recommendations.

The war in China intensified as Secretary of State George C. Marshall still held hopes that Wedemeyer could convince Chiang Kai-shek to institute the internal reforms Marshall believed necessary to win the support of the Chinese people. But that didn't happen. The Communists led by Mao captured the Chinese mainland in 1949 and Chiang was forced to retreat with his forces and supporters into exile on the island of Formosa. His island redoubt is today the modern nation of Taiwan.

The loss of China to the Communists was a serious blow to American foreign policy — one which happened on Truman and Marshall's watch.

Wedemeyer went before Congress and blamed the defeat on Truman's failure to continue training and modernizing the Nationalist forces. The Truman Administration attributed the loss to the extremely low morale extant in China, the result of Chiang's corrupt and oppressive regime. Those conditions, said Marshall, deprived the people of the spirit and will to fight against the Communist onslaught.

Both Wedemeyer and Marshall were partially right. But the conservative wing of the Republican party blamed Marshall for the "loss of China".

On June 14, 1951, while the Korean War raged, Senator Joseph R. McCarthy gave a major speech before the United States Senate in which he declared that Wedemeyer had prepared a wise plan for keeping China a valued ally but that it had been sabotaged by the Truman Administration. Had his epic address of three hours been confined to criticism of the Democratic Administration's policies, it would have likely been viewed as statesman — like and might have attracted only temporary attention. But McCarthy went way beyond mere policy differences in crossing over into the realm of harsh and bitter personal attacks and recriminations.

"Only in treason," announced McCarthy, "can we find why evil genius thwarted and frustrated it." (i.e. Wedemeyer's plan). "The evil geniuses," McCarthy declared, included General George C. Marshall; and "if Marshall were merely stupid," McCarthy added "the laws of probability would dictate that part of his decisions would serve this country's interests." Referring to General Marshall as a "grim and solitary man," McCarthy accused the highly respected soldier-statesman of being "at the heart of a conspiracy on a scale so immense as to dwarf any previous such venture in the history of man.[1]"

Marshall had earlier been vilified as "a living lie" by McCarthy's close colleague and Chairman of the Senate Internal Security Subcommittee, Senator William E. Jenner of Indiana.

---

[1] A History of the American People, Vol. II, by Paul Johnson (Easton Press, 1997) page 836.

McCarthy's attack on Marshall came as a great shock to Eisenhower, and to much of the nation. Marshall had been Ike's mentor, partner in victory and boss. He had also been the navigator of Eisenhower's career through the late 30's and early 40's. Ike was Marshall's hand-picked man to lead the great alliance which fought Hitler to his destruction. In his position as Army Chief of Staff, George Marshall was President Roosevelt's chief military strategist and adviser. Roosevelt was so dependent upon Marshall that he refused to let him leave Washington to command the Allies himself. So Marshall, a humble man, invested his full faith in Eisenhower. It was a one hundred percent professional commitment. Marshall liked Ike and, therefore, so did FDR. And after Roosevelt died before the war was over, his successor, Harry S. Truman, also placed his faith in Marshall. It would not be hyperbole to state that a semblance of a father-son relationship had slowly developed between Marshall and Eisenhower during the pre-war years and World War II.

To the American public, the taciturn Marshall was far from a cult hero. Unlike Eisenhower he was wanting in natural political skills. But still, a majority of Americans greatly admired his abilities and character. Marshall was highly respected for the roles he played in the Allied victory in WW II and the saving of Western Europe from Communism through the Marshall Plan and the Berlin Airlift.

Had McCarthy's comments been made in more temperate times, they would likely have held little currency with the American people and been dismissed as either pure demagoguery or pure nonsense. But the summer of 1951 was hardly a normal time. McCarthy's accusations of a year and a half earlier of 205 Communists in the State Department had strongly resonated with a restive American public already traumatized by the recent Communist takeover of China; the explosion of an atomic bomb by Russia in 1949 and the revelation of traitors in their midst who had allegedly fed the Soviet Union America's atomic secrets.

Never mind that McCarthy changed the number of Communists from 205 to 57, the day after he made the claim, and thereafter could never seem to settle on a number. He sensed that his accusations had hit pay dirt. A steady drumbeat of allegations and revelations — most of them spurious, such as the charges against Owen

Lattimore[2], followed, till reaching a crescendo with McCarthy's June 1951 Senate speech vilifying George Marshall, by then an embattled and physically depleted Secretary of Defense presiding over the unpopular Korean War.

But the American people were vulnerable in 1951. Their psyches were malleable. The shock of learning that distinguished New Dealers who had held positions of trust in the State Department and other branches of government, such as Alger Hiss and Harry Dexter White, were Communists or "Fellow Travelers" who had engaged in treasonous acts, had already weakened many Americans' natural resistance to sensational charges.

McCarthy burst onto the American scene at just the right time for him and his supporters. There was nothing special or extraordinary about the man. If it had not been him, it might have been someone else who instinctively seized and exploited the fact that vast numbers of U.S. citizens had temporarily taken their healthy skepticism, placed it on a shelf and then locked the closet door. Instead of "McCarthyism," the phenomenon might have been known as "Jennerism" or "Knowlandism". But it was McCarthy who emerged in 1950 as the guidon bearer for the new anti-communism. It was his star which shot with white hot intensity into the heavens, only to gradually lose its incandescence, until burning out and crashing to Earth with a thud by the end of 1954.

In 1951 and 1952, however, McCarthy's stock was at its peak and legions of normally cautious Americans found themselves all-in, and buying high.

That McCarthy would ultimately besmirch the good name of anti-communism seemed a fanciful idea in 1951, a notion held only by his most implacable foes.

It would be a disservice to the truth, however, to posit that the principal cause of McCarthyism was McCarthy. Such a facile and superficial theorem would fly in the face of the facts of the corrosive

---

[2] Pace, Eric, New York Times, 6/1/89: Owen Lattimore was a State Department consultant and China expert accused by Senator McCarthy of being "the top Russian espionage agent in the United States." After many official investigations, the charges remained unsubstantiated.

era of history — perhaps two decades in length — which produced McCarthyism as a toxic by-product. Because, despite some extreme liberal bias to the contrary, the factual foundation for the anti-Red scare was real. That the lead actors, however, on the stage of the anti-communist theater, were men like Joseph McCarthy and William Jenner was akin to Frank Sinatra in the role of Hamlet with Dean Martin as Horatio.

Communist penetration of America's institutions took hold during the great Depression of the 1930's. Many of Franklin D. Roosevelt's New Dealers — bureaucrats and intellectuals — were radicalized by what they believed had been the root cause of the world-wide Depression: unchecked capitalism run amuck. It took only a short leap from there to adopt the socialist teachings of Marx and Lenin. Many joined the Socialist or Communist Parties in America. Some betrayed their country by becoming spies for the Soviet Union. They used their gilt-edge résumés and squeaky clean reputations. As the cadre of the United States group of new young leaders, they penetrated and became embedded in the State Department, the Department of the Treasury, the Agricultural Adjustment Administration; the Department of War, Navy and Justice and even the OSS.[3]

Among the more prominent Americans who were believed to be actively engaged in espionage for the Soviet Union as members of Communist cells were Whittaker Chambers, former Editor-in-Chief of Time Magazine; Alger Hiss, a high level State Department official; Maurice Halperin, an OSS Section Chief; Donald Hiss, an official of the Department of the Interior; Elizabeth Bentley and Harry Dexter White.

No less a prominent personage than George Kennan, U.S. Ambassador to Russia in the 1940's and author of America's policy of "containment," admitted in his memoirs that the "penetration of American governmental services by members or agents (conscious or otherwise) of the American Communist Party, was not a figment

---

[3] Alger Hiss: Why He Chose Treason by Cristina Shelton (Threshold Editions, 2012) p. 82.

of the imagination but really existed and assumed proportions which, while never overwhelming, were also not trivial."[4]

George Kennan, possessed of a fiercely independent bent of mind, was no knee-jerk anything. Though his peers, such as close friend and colleague Paul Nitze, might disagree with Kennan from time to time, no one could honestly disparage the quality of his intellect and the rigor of his scholarly discipline. Tellingly, Kennan believed that the Roosevelt Administration was remiss in failing to heed the warnings about the extent of Communist activity in the U.S. Government.[5]

It is now an historical fact that the U.S. Government's perceived protective wall of security against hostile subversion was breached in many places and seriously penetrated by Soviet Intelligence Services during the 1930's and 40's. Foremost among those services were the GRU (Soviet Army Intelligence) and later the KGB.[6]

It is also an historical fact that in America of the 1930's and 40's, there existed a group of opinion-makers outside of government and policy-makers within — relatively few in number but impressive in their degree of influence — who were committed proponents of Marxist-Leninist doctrine. Some were active members of the Communist Party in America; others were socialists or communist-sympathizers. Some simply espoused Communism; others practiced it. In its least noxious form this consisted of attempting to advance pro-Soviet policies within the Department of State and Defense. At its most virulent and dangerous; it manifested itself in espionage, subversion and treason.

With the Soviet Union as one the U.S.'s principal allies in World War II, the patriotic fervor which engulfed the American people in their quest to defeat the fascist governments of Germany, Japan and Italy, had made many Americans more tolerant of the Soviet Union. During the years 1941 through 1945 Stalin's communist regime took on an aura approaching respectability in America's consciousness.

---

[4] A History of The American People, Ibid, p. 833.
[5] A History of The American People, Id.
[6] Alger Hiss, Why He Chose Treason, Ibid, p. 82; citing also "The New Dealers War: FDR and the War Within WW II by Thomas Fleming, pp. 319-20.

War and hatred of the Nazis, combined with a determination to unconditionally defeat the Japan which had attacked Pearl Harbor, temporarily deluded large segments of the nation into believing, that Stalin and his repressive regime weren't all that bad.

Of course, these illusions could not last long as they passed through the filter of America's good sense during the post-war years. Beginning in late 1945 and through 1950, America underwent a metamorphosis in how it viewed Soviet Russia and its satellites. During those years the Soviet Union was transformed from America's ally to its enemy. And Joe McCarthy and his cohorts had little to do with it.

The Soviet Union itself created the powerful anti-communist sentiment in the United States. It accomplished this by word and deed — by its ruthless domination of Eastern Europe, by the Berlin Blockade, by deadly purges and show-trials, by man-made famine in selected regions of its empire, by the gulag, the theft of U.S. atomic secrets leading to the explosion of its own A-bomb in 1949, and by instigating the Korean War in 1950.

So decisive was America's conversion into a foe of the U.S.S.R. that forty years after the end of World War II, an American President, Ronald Reagan, could call it an "evil empire" with nary a single dissenting voice to be heard.

The only truly remarkable thing about Joseph McCarthy was not his popularity and power during the period of 1950 through much of 1954, but rather that it lasted for so short a period of time.

While William F. Buckley's "McCarthy and His Enemies" gathered attention in some quarters of America's intelligentsia in the '50s, the essential truth was that McCarthy's greatest enemy was himself.

Perhaps failing to grasp the irony of his actions, McCarthy worked at cross-purposes with his message. He somehow failed to grasp the most basic fact that by employing many of the same methods used by the communist propaganda machine — such as the "big lie", character assassination, willfully false accusations, innuendo, and recklessness as to people's rights — he slowly but steadily cut the high ground out from under his feet.

McCarthy achieved early spectacular success but over a five-year period slowly self-destructed as he repeatedly offended America's innate sense of fairness.

As Dwight D. Eisenhower, however, planned the first midwest leg of his campaign in the late summer of 1952, Senator Joseph R. McCarthy was a force to be reckoned with. Eisenhower himself was a strong anti-communist but the danger of internal subversion in 1952 was simply not as acute as it had been in April of 1945, when FDR died suddenly in Warms Springs, Georgia. Even accounting for the fact that Roosevelt's first concern was winning the war — with Soviet Russia an essential cog in the allies' war machine — he still paid far less attention to Communist infiltration of the U.S. government than was defensible.

The Truman Administration, unshackled from the chains of war after August of 1945, was far more diligent[7]. Even at the apex of his career as an internationalist, Truman was still a quintessential son of the conservative midwest, which carried with it an inbred-mistrust of Eastern establishment — particularly Ivy League — intellectuals, such as those who carried their leftist ideologies into the Departments of State and Defense in the 30s and early 40s.

By breeding, tradition and genetics, Truman was a steel-edged populist when it came to domestic policy. Foreign policy was another matter. He had no illusions about Stalin and Molotov and kept them at a distance at the Potsdam Summit Conference in the summer of 1945. And Churchill's chilling admonition to the world in 1946 that an "iron curtain" had descended upon Eastern Europe jolted Truman's view of international communism even more.

In November of 1946, Truman embarked on a campaign of vigilance to thwart domestic subversion. The first step was his appointment of a Temporary Commission of Employee Loyalty. The following March he acted upon its recommendation by issuing Executive Order 9835 which authorized inquiries into the political beliefs and associations of all federal employees.

From a purely political standpoint, Truman was forced to take visible action. He faced a tough reelection campaign in 1948 no

[7] A History of the American People, Id. P. 833.

matter who the Republican candidate happened to be. In 1946 and into 1947, a "Red Scare" permeated America. Writing for the Washington Post in 1947, Edward T. Folliard found "hatred of communism rampant" everywhere he traveled[8].

Under pressure from Attorney General Thomas Clark, Truman authorized a continuation of electronic surveillance in cases where national defense was involved.

Serving as a reminder to Truman as to just how vulnerable Democrats were to "soft on communism" charges, was the constant drumbeat of Representative J. Parnell Thomas of New Jersey, the Chairman of the House Committee on Un-American activities. Seeking to steal some of H.U.A.C.'s thunder, if not pre-empting it entirely on the issue of loyalty in government, Truman established an elaborate Federal Employees Loyalty and Security Program. "I am not worried about the Communist Party taking over the government of the United States," said Truman, "but I am against a person whose loyalty is not to the government of the United States holding a government job."[9]

Within a few months, the FBI began running name checks on every one of the 2 million people on the federal payrolls. Three million would be cleared by 1951 by the FBI and Civil Service Commission. Several thousand more would resign. Only 212 federal employees were dismissed as being of questionable loyalty. Yet in a Lincoln Day Speech in Wheeling West Virginia in February of 1950, McCarthy spoke of 205 Communists in the State Department. Typically, he got his information wrong. There was no list of 205 names. McCarthy plucked the number 205 from a letter written by Secretary of State James Byrnes a few years earlier. He never had any actual names.

The Republicans in Congress had for the most part concluded by the end of 1951, that Harry Truman was no pushover when it came to communism. Despite scathing criticism throughout most of his presidency — which pretty much coincided with the heightened level of the Red Scare — Truman managed by the end of his

---

[8] Truman, by David McCullough, Touchstone, 1992, p. 521.
[9] Id, p. 552.

administration in January of 1953 to deflect the worst of the verbal brick bats thrown his way over softness on communism, while burnishing his own credentials as an anti-communist at the same time.

Truman's offensive against disloyalty and sedition in government created a curious anomaly. Those who spied for ideological reasons were mostly eliminated while those who spied for money continued to have a firm foot-hold in the espionage trade.[10] This may have been more a testament to the ever-enduring profit motive in the affairs of men than to any particular ineffectiveness in Truman's program.

Truman's modicum of success, however, in no way exonerated the Roosevelt and Truman Administrations in the eyes of the Republican opposition — especially in Congress. As far as they were concerned, weak Democratic policies vis a vís the infiltration by Communist subversives of U.S. institutions, had resulted in the loss of Eastern Europe, and then the loss of China.

At the end of the day, the Truman Administration could point to some solid accomplishments in its war against Communist subversion and espionage. On January 11, 1950, a mere fortnight before McCarthy gave his 205 communists in the State Department speech, Alger Hiss in his retrial in Federal District Court, was convicted of perjury for lying about being a communist agent (The Statute of Limitations had run on espionage charges). On December 9, 1950 Harry Gold was convicted on spy charges. He and co-defendants, David and Ruth Greenglass, confessed their guilt. David Greenglass, Ethel Rosenberg's brother turned state's evidence, implicating Julius and Ethel Rosenberg in espionage. They were convicted and executed in 1953. Another co-conspirator, Martin Sobell, was also convicted.

There is no known evidence that Senator McCarthy "ever identified any subversive not already known to the authorities."[11] This is an accurate statement but history compels a caveat. Despite the distress caused by McCarthy to many innocent people, there is

---

[10] Id.
[11] Id. at 835.

also no known evidence that his anti-communist crusade did not deter would-be subversives from engaging in nefarious activities. And whether he created a positive environment of enhanced vigilance in America against internal enemies, cannot be answered with an unequivocal no. It remains, as always, as difficult to prove a negative as to disprove an intangible.

One thing about which there can be little debate is that as the twilight of the Truman presidency descended over the Potomac in the Fall of 1952, it was Dwight D. Eisenhower's turn to march into the fire.

CHAPTER THREE

In Silent Contempt

Republican presidential candidate Dwight D. Eisenhower, stated unequivocally concerning Joseph McCarthy, "I despise his tactics."[12] But, Eisenhower was not greatly perturbed by public comments from McCarthy, such as his telegram to Harry S. Truman in 1950 which declared that there were "57 card-carrying Communists or loyal to the Communist Party" in the State Department[13]. Eisenhower was well familiar with the types of political utterances of high-profile figures, drenched in hyperbole and bordering on prevarication. From 1942 through 1945 he skillfully managed a host of powerful men far more clever than McCarthy. His deft handling of larger-than-life individuals such as Churchill, de Gaulle, Montgomery and Patton held a coalition together, which was no small part of the formula for victory in the war in Western Europe.

Eisenhower was neither a military theorist nor a political philosopher. His special genius was grounded in an awareness of a

---

[12] Eisenhower letter to Paul Roy Helms, Eisenhower Presidency, Wikipedia, p. 28.
[13] The Fifties, by David Halberstam, (Villard Books, 1953) p. 151.

group of bedrock human traits which he called "subjects that touch the soul": beliefs, aspirations ideals and hatreds, all of which Eisenhower knew needed to be seriously addressed if one wanted to be a successful leader.[14] And Eisenhower had no peers when it came to the sophisticated management of a multinational command dominated by prima donnas..."[15] His skillful handling of powerful men led to assessments like the following: "Behind his open smile, Eisenhower was a secretive and subtle leader of quiet moral courage — a brilliant intellectual tactician but also a master of calculated duplicity."[16]

The type of slanderous character assassination directed by McCarthy and his followers, such as Senators Jenner of Indiana and Knowland of California, were another matter entirely. The reputations being savaged and destroyed included those of some men who Eisenhower greatly respected. Foremost among them was George C. Marshall. When William Jenner, Chairman of Senate Internal Security Committee, added to McCarthy's accusation that Marshall was an anti-American conspirator, the charge that Ike's wartime mentor was "a living lie",[17] the bile of disgust which rose in Eisenhower's throat choked him with rage.

The outrageous behavior, however, was coming from influential members of Eisenhower's own party whose active support he might need to get elected as president. This presented him with a particularly thorny dilemma.

With his legendary self-control, Eisenhower attempted to bottle up his exasperation. An exception to his silent contempt was his explosion to his staff about Knowland of California, of whom Eisenhower said, "he confounded the age-old question of 'How stupid can you get?'"[18]

Compounding the problem was Truman's swift and fierce defense of Marshall as one of the greatest of all Americans, which

---

[14] The Guns at Last Light, by Rick Atkinson, Review by Dennis Showalter, History, (History Book Club) Late Spring 2013, p. 2.
[15] Id, at 3.
[16] Ike's Bluff, by Evan Thomas (Little Brown & Co., 2012).
[17] Murrow by A.M. Sperber (Freundlick Books, 1987) p. 388.
[18] The Fifties, Id at 56.

the feisty president reprised at every opportunity. If Truman could defend and extol a man who merely served in his cabinet, could Eisenhower do any less for the same man who had chosen him for greatness and mentored his meteoric rise from obscurity during World War II?

A further complicating factor was that Marshall, with his typical blend of self-approbation and modesty, felt no compulsion to defend himself. He repeatedly refused to respond to McCarthy's charges, declaring that, "if at this time in my career, I have to prove I'm not a traitor, it's hardly worth it."[19] In the eyes of much of the press and public, such admirable self-restraint imposed a special duty upon those public figures closest to Marshall to come to his defense. Eisenhower would find no absolution in the fact that Marshall had asked no one to defend him. Described as "a stoic man with an overwhelming sense of personal duty and marginal expectation of the political process,"[20] Marshall remarked to his goddaughter with understated irony that "there was no more political independence in politics than there was in jail."[21]

To presidential nominee Eisenhower, Marshall's grace under attack, only increased by geometric progression his personal imperative to speak up for the man whose relationship with Ike was described by his close aide, Harry Butcher, as that "of father and son."[22]

More than a decade later when Eisenhower was free from political pressures, he expressed his true feelings about McCarthy and McCarthyism in his memoirs of his first four year term as president titled Mandate for Change[23]:

> "Senator McCarthy's general and specific allegations were, from the start, so extreme, often involving unsupported and unjustified

[19] The Smithsonian Channel, special on Joseph R. McCarthy, broadcast 12/26/12.
[20] The Fifties, Id., p. 251.
[21] Id.
[22] Id.
[23] Mandate For Change, 1953-1956, Dwight D. Eisenhower (Doubleday) 1963, p. 316.

allegations of the gravest kind, that his attacks,
which at times degenerated to persecution,
became known as "McCarthyism."

Although theretofore diffident about it, there is little doubt that by the summer of 1952, Eisenhower was appalled at the way in which his revered mentor, George C. Marshall, had been "persecuted". As soon as his nomination was official, he intended to rush to Marshall's aid at the first opportunity. Unfortunately, a combination of circumstances and perhaps his own lack of moral will power began conspiring against him shortly after his nomination on July 10, 1952, and undermining his best intentions.

In his memoirs, Eisenhower decried the fact that McCarthy, "protected as he was by congressional immunity" could attack anyone at any time with impunity. Eisenhower recalled how among educators, the press, and the clergy-indeed all informed groups the question was often — and justifiably — asked, "Who is safe?"[24]

From the time of his nomination, however, in July of 1952 to Inauguration Day in January of 1953, a gathering storm of resentment between Ike and Truman cast its dark shadows incrementally; and slowly engulfed and shattered their relationship. Once again one did not have to look beyond McCarthyism to find the seeds of the feud. So emotionally affected were both men by McCarthy's conduct and its larger implications for the November elections — between Eisenhower and Truman's favorite, Adlai Stevenson — that the outspoken Truman seemed unable to stop himself from harshly criticizing Eisenhower for not being outspoken enough against McCarthyism. And Ike came to deeply resent the criticism, which he viewed as absurdly excessive in the light of political realities. By the time Ike's limousine pulled up to the White House to pick up the outgoing president and First Lady on Inauguration Day, the two men were barely speaking.

Thus, it is vastly revealing as to how profound Ike's animus against McCarthy was, that in his memoirs he went out of his way to throw a bouquet to Truman related to the very topic which had

---

[24] Id.

severed their relationship in 1952 — McCarthyism. The historically meaningful statement is contained in one sentence written by Eisenhower in <u>Mandate for Change</u> in 1963: "Ironically, as it has been suggested, it (i.e. McCarthy's false charge of 205 card-carrying Communists in the State Department) might well have been forgotten if the Truman administration had not challenged it, demanding that he produce his source of information or quit talking."[25]

But the clarity of Ike's retrospective of 1963 was wanting in his resolve of 1952. Missing were the bold strokes and sharp incisions of the kind found in his memoirs. It was not a question of not knowing what he should do. That much was clear. Even his opponent for the Republican nomination for president, Senator Robert A. Taft of Ohio, a midwestern conservative, had "refused to embrace all of McCarthy's charges, in particular the assault on General Marshall."[26]

Eisenhower had clear opportunities in the weeks following his nomination to take on the group of midwestern and far western isolationists in the Republican Party, referred to by Dean Acheson, as "the primitives"[27]. But perhaps because he was an inexperienced novice when it came to national politics, certain truisms seemed to elude his attention or full comprehension. For one thing, although McCarthy was still a colossus of politics in America — a menace to almost anyone against whom charges of being soft on Communism might stick — Ike was as close to being the teflon national figure as anyone else in American history. His aura was that of a modern-day Zeus. He was the all-conquering hero to two hundred million Americans and countless Europeans as well. Short of planning the violent overthrow of the U.S. Government, Eisenhower was immune from criticism in the eyes of most Americans. Contrast Ike's exalted position to that of McCarthy and the latter comes up short. By the time Eisenhower was inaugurated, three years by McCarthy, of endless charges with very little proof to back them up, were wearing

[25] Id.
[26] <u>Eisenhower and the anti-Communist Crusade</u> by Jeff Broadwater (University of North Carolina Press, 1992) p. 26.
[27] <u>The Fifties</u>, Id., p. 56.

thin."[28] A pimple on the path of progress" was one of the more colorful epithets Eisenhower employed in describing McCarthy.[29] Regrettably, during the presidential and congressional campaigns of 1952, Ike underestimated the extent of his own clout and cachet with the American people; while McCarthy overestimated his.

McCarthy mistook his usefulness to his colleagues for their genuine respect and admiration. Fellow midwestern senator, John Bricker of Ohio, is reported to have said to McCarthy, "Joe, you're a real SOB...but sometimes it's useful to have SOBs around to do the dirty work."[30] McCarthy failed to comprehend that his true value to the Republican Party was not catching traitors and spies. He should have understood this because he wasn't catching any. His real value was in "allowing worthier men to keep their hands clean."[31]

As the July sunshine glimmered off the presidential monuments, Washington, D.C. was abuzz with questions: Would Ike back Joe for re-election? It seemed almost a certainty that in some form he would. The better question being asked was, Would Ike do anything about McCarthyism?[32] The "old guard" of the Republican Party, composed of men such as Charles Halleck, Everett Dirkson, Henry Cabot Lodge, Paul G. Hoffman and Leonard Hall, were of little help to Eisenhower in answering the questions. They were essentially pragmatic men, more interested in Ike's election than the deeper moral and policy issues posed by the political pandemic called McCarthyism.

Ike himself was conflicted. In September he phoned campaign secretary, James C. Hagerty, from his Gettysburg farm and decried the fact that he was receiving such strong pressure from the Old Guard to make the already planned but debated campaign swing through Wisconsin as a "healing gesture" to McCarthy and his wing

---

[28] Id. p. 50.
[29] Id.
[30] Id. p. 250. John Bricker authored the so-called Bricker Amendments seeking to limit the Executive Branch's authority to enter into foreign treaties and alliances. They were defeated by the Eisenhower Administration.
[31] Id.
[32] The Nightmare Decade: The Life & Times of Joe McCarthy, by Fred. J. Cook, (Random House, 1971) p. 383.

of the party.[33] Ike conveyed his serious reservations about making his first campaign trip, through the heartland of Republican conservatism and hotbed of strident McCarthyism.[34] And, what's more, they wanted him to back both Jenner and McCarthy for re-election. A perturbed Eisenhower instructed Hagerty to organize a Campaign Committee meeting for mid-September at the Manhattan residence of New York Governor Thomas E. Dewey, a party moderate.[35] Ike's consternation had become more acute after an early September Republican Party rally in Indianapolis where he appeared with Senator William E. Jenner, a man he abhorred.

At the meeting, Dewey — a former crime-busting prosecutor with an impeccable legal pedigree — was vocal in urging Eisenhower to resist pressure to visit Wisconsin. Dewey's contempt for McCarthy was palpable. Possessed of a finely honed sensibility as to the rule of law and the high standards of proof required in court to label one a traitor or a conspirator, Dewey was appalled by McCarthy's irresponsibility concerning individuals' reputations and lives. Dewey himself had been verbally attacked by Senator Everett Dirkson of Illinois in a speech at the 1952 Republican Convention for leading the party down the path to destruction in his unsuccessful efforts as the party's standard-bearer in the 1944 and 1948 presidential elections.

Dewey's counsel, however, was outweighed by that of other advisers.[36] While Ike shared Dewey's enmity towards McCarthy, he was also a shrewd player in the game of survival. Otherwise, he would never have reached the pinnacles of success achieved in both military and civilian life. Eisenhower knew the risks of tangling with a McCarthy. But Ike was certainly not risk-averse. His decision to launch the allied invasion of Normandy on June 6, 1944 after days of terrible weather was extremely risky. But the decision was a

---

[33] Eisenhower & the Anti-Communist Crusade, Id. p. 39.
[34] Id.
[35] Id., p. 44.
[36] Id. Among those advisers who agreed with Governor Dewey, there was the feeling that McCarthy strongly opposed Eisenhower's points of view on the right to civil liberties, particularly the rights of assembly and free speech, as well as all his legislative positions and that, therefore, he owed McCarthy nothing.

calculated risk. Before iterating the famous words, "Let's go," he carefully weighed the opinions of all his top people, including Bradley and Montgomery, and made sure his weather experts were reasonably sure that an expected break in the bad weather would afford a window of opportunity to launch the D-Day invasion.

Eisenhower would be no less cautious in answering the vexing questions about McCarthy. In his memoirs, he stated that initially, "I told my staff to make no plans for visiting Wisconsin...I was determined to give no appearance of aligning my views with his."[37] Yet, on the same page, Eisenhower wrote that he "would be expected to support all Republican candidates for office."[38] He also related his version of how the mid-western campaign trip came about:

> "Later while I was preoccupied with the daily demands of strenuous political campaigning, itineraries for my traveling were fixed before I became aware that they provided for a tour through Wisconsin, with a number of whistle stops and one formal speaking engagement."[39]

Just when it was that Eisenhower first became aware of the planned Wisconsin trip is a question mired in history's contradictions. Certainly he must have known by the time he returned to New York from Denver in late August.

Beneath Eisenhower's placid exterior was a trigger for volatility. Though generally calm, he could, when provoked, unleash a fierce temper. General George Patton was one of those who experienced Ike's wrath first-hand when he made politically incorrect remarks in a speech in England during the early planning for D-day. Though the timing is unclear, there is little doubt that Ike also blew his stack at some point after learning of the planned campaign trip to Wisconsin. The eruption of anger was apparently directed more at his hands-on campaign people than at his top advisors. Whenever it

---

[37] <u>Mandate for Change</u>, Id., p. 317.
[38] <u>Id.</u>
[39] Id.

was, Ike was furious[40]: "This occasioned the sharpest flare-up I can recall between my staff and I during the entire campaign." His reaction is not surprising. Ike instinctively recoiled from anything having to do with McCarthy. He wrote eloquently about his feelings in Mandate For Change and left no doubt as to how profoundly they were rooted in his fundamental principles:

> "...he (McCarthy) too often forgot the complex and precious American issues of personal liberties and constitutional process; and he all too frequently ignored the incalculably important doctrine of the relationship between the Legislative and Executive branches."[41]

Eisenhower had decisively concluded by the time of the 1952 Republican Convention that McCarthy's avowed purpose of fighting Communism had "become hopelessly entangled with, and frustrated by his methods."[42] "It was his methods," said Ike, "that were labeled as McCarthyism."[43]

Eisenhower's eruption of anger was by his estimation not the consequence of embarrassment of having to meet publicly with McCarthy on the latter's home turf. Rather, he ultimately blamed the bad strategy of the move as the source of his ire:

> "For two reasons, the blunder rankled. The first was that either attitude I might take — refusal on the one hand to brawl publicly with McCarthy in his own state or, on the other, refusal to imply personal acquiescence in his methods — could create unfortunate political division in Wisconsin and lend further currency and power to his charges. The second reason was nothing more than frustration that my

---

[40] Id.
[41] Id. p. 321.
[42] Id.
[43] Id.

specific instructions had been overlooked and a speaking program so definitely arranged that it was now impossible for me to repudiate it. I was caught in a position that allowed no alternative."[44]

After the meeting with Dewey and the other advisers, there seemed to be no turning back from the mid-western trip; but if Ike was going to campaign in McCarthy's back yard, it would be on his terms. He called a staff meeting to be held at his Morningside Heights apartment; acquired by him when he was president of Columbia University.

Among those to attend the meeting would be Sherman Adams, James C. Hagerty, C. D. Jackson, and Emmett John Hughes.

As Eisenhower gazed out upon the majestic Hudson River from one of his favorite secluded spots near the Cloisters Museum, the short history of the most recent events in the McCarthy controversy surged like a wild river current through his brain. He had come to this upper Manhattan spot to think; and the small Secret Service detail assigned to him kept out of sight.

Ike had been to this location in moments of decision many times and the spectacular view of the river from on-high never ceased to inspire him and dispel the dark clouds of doubt from the horizon. Some of his heroes of American history were connected to the mighty Hudson, particularly General George Washington who escaped from New York City with his army across the Hudson in 1776 and then had to bear witness to an attack upon the Continental Army's cliff-top redoubt on the Hudson and its surrender to the British. Musing upon these monumental battles of the American Revolution on or near the Hudson River seemed to strengthen Ike's resolve. Thus, it was a renewed Eisenhower who directed his campaign staff meeting later that day. But first as he gazed over the river at the steep palisades on the New Jersey side, his powers of memory and thought were at their apogee.

---

[44] Id., p. 317.

Dwight D. Eisenhower (18901969)
Presidential Photo Portrait

Advisers Henry Cabot Lodge and Herbert Brownell had advised Eisenhower in the late spring to ignore McCarthy in the campaign and focus on the Democrats' failures in national security and foreign policy. This strategy would not only allow him to sharply contrast their ineptitude in the areas of internal security and China, with his stellar performance in defeating the Axis Powers in Europe, but would give him an independent voice, free of McCarthy's demagoguery. Thus, Ike's political speeches in June of 1952 sounded a drum beat of criticism of the last two Democratic administrations. There was a third collateral benefit. Ike was successfully able to portray himself as an internationalist as opposed to his presidential rival Senator Robert Taft, who was widely viewed as an isolationist.

Ike continued in this vein at the Republican national convention during the week of July 7, 1952 — ignoring McCarthyism while drawing sharp lines of difference between himself and Taft. His well-conceived personal platform provided momentum for the successful launch into the presidential campaign.

On August 22, 1952 at a press conference in Denver, Eisenhower refused to give McCarthy a blanket endorsement for re-election to the U.S. Senate. In an example of Ike's vaunted craftiness he allowed that he would support the Wisconsin Senator "as a member of the Republican organization."[45]

With his rapier wit, Democratic Nominee Adlai Stevenson ridiculed Ike's trapeze act as a "middle of the gutter approach."[46]

Be that as it may, the Denver press conference was a dramatic success for Eisenhower. He was flying high, buoyed by the unique platform afforded him. Asked by reporters about McCarthy and McCarthyism, the Republican candidate responded with force and eloquence: "I am not going to support anything that smacks to me of un-American — that is un-American in character, and that includes any kind of thing that looks to me like unjust damaging of reputation, where the man has not the usual recourse to law."[47] Then, with his sails unfurled and a strong wind at his back, an exuberant Eisenhower used a reporter's question concerning the attacks on General Marshall to launch a pointed defense of his mentor. Quickly stepping from behind his desk and taking up a position in the center of the room, Eisenhower held forth with emotion: "There is nothing of disloyalty in General Marshall's

---

[45] Eisenhower and the Anti-Communist Crusade, Id., p. 37.
[46] Id., p. 44.
[47] The Nightmare Decade: Id., p. 383

soul...he is a man of real selflessness...a perfect example of patriotism and loyal servant of the United States."

It was with a sense of triumph that the Republican candidate returned to New York. But like many other vicissitudes of life — no less so in politics — the spirit of Denver would not last long. No one, however, could have predicted just how far Ike would fall from the moral high ground of Denver, over the next two months.

The first flap involved his planned campaign trip to the mid-west. The Eisenhower Campaign had originally scheduled his visit to Wisconsin for September 5, 1952. This date, only four days before the scheduled Republican primary, was designed to allow Ike to get in and out of Wisconsin quickly without endorsing anyone — most especially McCarthy. And the flip side was he would also avoid "having to endure the political embrace of Joe McCarthy."[48] The Wisconsin Republican Machine, however, cried foul. They bluntly told the Eisenhower campaign to stay out of the State until after the Primary.[49] One can certainly appreciate their concerns given Ike's tepid and ambivalent posture concerning their flagship candidate, Senator Joseph McCarthy. The Eisenhower people yielded but it was too late for them to cancel the first leg of the trip to Indiana.

The Wisconsin primary on September 9, 1952 was a resounding triumph for McCarthy, outdrawing all other candidates combined — Republicans and Democrats — on a record voter turnout. Not so for Eisenhower. As Wisconsin Republican voters were selecting their party's nominees for Congress, Eisenhower was unhappily campaigning in Indiana alongside Senator William Jenner, also running for re-election. At this early stage of his political life Eisenhower had not reached the peak of his personal animosity toward McCarthy. His feelings towards Jenner, however, were unequivocal. He found the man repulsive and slimy.[50]

While September 9, 1952 was one of the best days in McCarthy's political career, for Eisenhower it was one of his worst. Also seeking

---

[48] Id.
[49] Id.
[50] Eisenhower and the Anti-Communist Crusade, Id., p. 42.

re-election, Senator Jenner had not only slandered Marshall but had attacked Eisenhower as well, as recently as late July, 1952.[51]

Appearing with Jenner on the same platform in Indianapolis at a highly publicized Republican rally, Ike had deleted from his prepared text an assertion that his administration would "not tolerate any trace of subversion or disloyalty in government office."[52] Eisenhower was not signaling any change of policy on internal security. He was simply withholding a huge piece of red meat for Jenner to feast upon that day. And he refused to endorse Jenner by name. But not so easily dismissed, the politically astute Jenner did wring from the Eisenhower people a commitment for Ike to introduce him so as to establish a political nexus between them; and then at the end of Eisenhower's speech, "seized the platform and grabbed Eisenhower's arm in a show of apparent unity."[53] "Charlie, get me out of here," Ike pleaded to Congressman Charles A. Halleck.[54]

Ike's closest aides could actually see him writhe under and recoil from Jenner's touch. His indignation continued unabated for the remainder of the day. Pulling aide Bernard M. Shanley aside, Ike fiercely whispered in his ear, "If Jenner puts his hand on me once again, I'm going to knock him right off the platform."[55]

Back in his Indianapolis hotel room, Eisenhower was "still almost purple with rage"[56] when one of his speech writers, Gabriel Hague, was called to meet with the candidate.

Now more than a week later as Ike gazed ruminatively across the Hudson River, most of his rage of Indianapolis had congealed into resolve. Disheartened by McCarthy's strong showing in the Wisconsin primary, almost all of Ike's advisers had come to believe that there was no politically strategic way to avoid a meeting with McCarthy on his home turf.

---

[51] Id.
[52] Id., p. 43.
[53] Id.
[54] Harry and Ike by Steve Neal (Scribner, 2001) p. 265.
[55] Id.
[56] Id., p. 43.

Eisenhower agreed but whether or not to go to Wisconsin was no longer his main focus — Since his jarring experience with Jenner, which he described as making him "feel dirty from the touch of the man,"[57] Eisenhower was truly excited at the prospect of purging from his system the toxicity caused by the incursions of the McCarthy-Jenner-Knowland cabal. The method he had chosen for his personal act of purification was a daring tribute to George C. Marshall "right in McCarthy's back yard."[58]

At the mid-September Morningside Heights staff meeting Eisenhower repressed as best he could the rage he still felt at suffering the embrace of Senator Jenner. And that memory, combined with how McCarthy had coasted to victory in the Wisconsin Primary, had made September 9th the toughest date of his campaign thus far.

"Jenner has called General Marshall 'a living lie' and Joe McCarthy has accused him of 'a monstrous conspiracy'[59]. Well I'm just not going to stand for it," announced the candidate.

"I understand the politics involved but that kind of 'ism' is despicable and has to be dealt with. Jenner even had the nerve to take some shots at us at the convention and McCarthy said nothing about it. Then you've got 'the top newspapers and organized labor' coming out against McCarthy in Wisconsin, yet he trounces the opposition anyway. You know what that does? It makes McCarthyism 'a political force to be reckoned with'[60] in other states besides Wisconsin — where candidates will adopt McCarthyism because it attracts votes."

Directing his attention to speech writer Emmett John Hughes, Ike ordered him to insert a defense of Marshall into a speech the candidate would deliver in Milwaukee "at the climax of the Wisconsin trip."[61] "I want the speech to make clear that these personal attacks are not the way freedom should defend itself."[62]

---

[57] The Nightmare Decade, Id., p. 384.
[58] Id.
[59] Murrow, His Life and Times by A.M. Sperber (Freundlick Books, 1986) p. 388.
[60] U.S. News and World Report, September 1952.
[61] Eisenhower and the Anti-Communist Crusade, Id., p. 45.
[62] Id.

The next day Hughes presented Eisenhower with the first draft of the speech containing the following paragraph:[63]

> "I know that charges of disloyalty have, in the past, been leveled against General George C. Marshall. I have been privileged for thirty-five years to know General Marshall personally. I know him, as a man and as a soldier, to be dedicated with singular selflessness and the profoundest patriotism to the service of America. And this episode is a sobering lesson of the way freedom must not defend itself."

Ike was pleased with the language on Marshall; his top advisers were less so. Several of them believed that Hughes's language "would cause an explosive and divisive effect..."[64] Eisenhower countered that he would "do it my way or I would cancel that part of the itinerary."[65]

Doing it his way, however, was not enough to impose discipline on Ike's advisers and supporters. He was no longer in the Army. Ignoring McCarthy's political shadow over the campaign was like ignoring the proverbial elephant in the room. By September 17, 1952, Senator Frank Carlson of Kansas, a top Eisenhower adviser, "was telling newsmen that Ike's managers were going to extend McCarthy an invitation to campaign widely outside his own state on the communists in government issue."[66] Eisenhower himself had agreed to no such thing. Only days later, things got worse when Senator Karl Mundt told the media that "Eisenhower would endorse and campaign actively for McCarthy."[67] In response, Campaign Secretary James C. Hagerty "commented cryptically, "The general speaks for himself.'"[68]

---

[63] The Fifties, Id. pp. 251 and 252.
[64] Mandate for Change, Id., p. 317.
[65] Id.
[66] The Nightmare Decade, Id., p. 384.
[67] Id., p. 383.
[68] Id.

It seemed that no one in Eisenhower's inner circle shared his passion and sense of moral imperative for repudiating McCarthy's virulent attacks on Marshall. On October 2, 1952, Eisenhower's train pulled out of Grand Central Station on the first leg of his trip to Wisconsin. Among the staffers and advisers on board was speech writer Emmett Hughes, who throughout the day worked with the candidate on multiple drafts of the planned Wisconsin speech, entitled, "Communism and Freedom." Ike warmed to the heavily thematic address as the day wore on. It was clear to Hughes and the other speech writers that the boss was treating this address as far more than just a political speech. Ike's fervor was contagious. His staff was abuzz with the excitement generated by the candidate's clear message that the speech was to be an historic exposition of the meaning of freedom. Its climax would be the declaration in defense of General Marshall, the man whom Ike believed had been foully maligned by McCarthy and Jenner.

Such noble impulses and spirited idealism seemed, however, to exist only aboard the train. Elsewhere fate's countervailing forces were hard at work at reversing Eisenhower's well-laid plan. It is now believed that someone in the Eisenhower camp leaked word of the tenor of the speech, because when the train pulled into Peoria, Illinois, where Ike and his people would spend the night, he was "besieged by national party officials and Wisconsin politicians urging him to delete the reference to Marshall from the speech.[69]

Eisenhower was unmoved and remained determined to deliver a ringing defense of Marshall in Milwaukee.

The proponents of expunging the defense of Marshall from the speech then stepped-up their assault by flying Joe McCarthy himself into Peoria to pay a surprise visit on the candidate. In Ike's hotel room, he and McCarthy "argued"[70] over the speech's content. Ike dug in his heels and McCarthy left in frustration but with no less determination to continue the battle.

---

[69] Eisenhower and the Anti-Communist Crusade, Id., p. 45.
[70] Id.

The next morning at breakfast, McCarthy told Eisenhower that "if he did not change his speech, he would be booed."[71] Leveling the same gaze into McCarthy's eyes that had caused the likes of Churchill and de Gaulle to back down, Ike replied: "I've been booed before, and being booed doesn't bother me."[72]

McCarthy, however, wasn't going to let Ike have the last word. The senator and his aides asked Ike's people if they could hitch a ride on their campaign train to Wisconsin. Backed into a corner, Eisenhower could hardly risk the tremendous fall-out which would ensue were he to deny McCarthy's request. Once on the train, McCarthy and his aides remonstrated with Ike's top advisers, presenting the consequences of Ike's tribute to Marshall on McCarthy's home turf in apocalyptic terms. McCarthy let the press, including the reporters on the train, know of his presence on board, thereby creating the impression of a close link to the national presidential campaign, which would make Ike's repudiation of McCarthy's attack on Marshall appear more divisive as it stood out in stark relief.

Finally, the man who may have been Eisenhower's most trusted adviser, former New Hampshire Governor Sherman Adams, asked to meet with him alone, whereupon he pleaded with the candidate to expunge the language concerning Marshall from the speech. Ike's inner circle were unanimous in urging him to drop the defense of Marshall.

Eisenhower, though furious, finally capitulated and agreed to the deletion.[73] Campaign staffers who were in Eisenhower's presence shortly after he acceded to his top advisers' request, described him as "glowering".[74]

The rest of Eisenhower's mid-west sojourn went straight downhill. His mood was dour. He was ashamed that he had caved in to the political pressure. Perhaps a more seasoned pro would have

---

[71] Id.
[72] Id.
[73] A copy of the sixth draft of the speech with the paragraph on George C. Marshall lined out is reproduced as attached Appendix A. It constitutes one of "The Presidential Papers of Dwight David Eisenhower" from the Eisenhower Presidential Library.
[74] Id., p. 45.

figured out a way to keep faith with his fellow Republicans, yet still get his point across. But Eisenhower did not. He was angry with his advisers and angry with the McCarthyites; but most of all he was angry with himself.

On the first stop, in Greenbay, Wisconsin, Ike informed his audience that although he and McCarthy had their differences, he wanted to be clear about one thing; "that the 'purposes' they both had of ridding the government of the incompetent, the dishonest and above all the subversive and disloyal were one of the same and they differed only over methods."[75] — as if to suggest that the methods Ike deplored as anti-American and anti-democratic were of minimal importance.

In later years Ike proffered something of a defense of his submissive behavior in Wisconsin by declaring, "I not only stated publicly (and privately) to him (i.e. McCarthy) that I disapproved of those methods, but I did so in his own state."[76]

On October 3, 1952, Ike delivered his long-anticipated speech in Milwaukee with Joseph McCarthy sitting nearby on the stage. Speaking over a coast to coast hook-up, he "assailed the poisoning of 'two decades of our national life' by 'a tolerance of communism,' and charging further 'the contamination in...every section of our government'[77]...a government of men whose very brains were confused by the opiate of this deceit...advisers in a foreign policy that...weakly bowed before the triumph in China of Communists...condoned the surrender of whole nations. It meant — in its most ugly triumph — treason itself."[78]

Eisenhower then shifted from the dire tone of the speech by attempting to introduce an element of balance and moderation. He called for "fairness" and the rights of fellow citizens to disagree."[79]

The Marshall paragraph was out and without it Eisenhower's tepid homage to fairness and the right to disagree, rang hollow.

---

[75] Murrow, Id., p. 389.
[76] The Presidency of Dwight David Eisenhower, Wikipedia.
[77] Murrow, Id.
[78] Murrow, Id.
[79] Id.

McCarthy took the credit for the purging of the Marshall defense, though substantial doubt exists that he ever saw a copy in advance.

Eisenhower's failure to come to the defense of Marshall was the product of "a decision that would haunt him for the rest of his life."[80] October 3, 1952 was one of the worst days of Eisenhower's political career. He was furious at McCarthy, his campaign advisers and himself. But, he alone had made the decision for reasons of political expediency, which had trumped decency, loyalty and principle. "Some of his oldest and closest friends, such as General Omar Bradley were appalled by his failure to defend Marshall."[81]

"'It turned my stomach,' Bradley wrote years later of Ike's failure to speak up for the man he had once revered, now that he was a political candidate. 'No man was more beholden to Marshall than Ike.'"

In New York, famed war correspondent and T.V. personality, Edward R. Murrow, screened the footage of Eisenhower's Milwaukee speech. As one of the country's most astute political observers, he instantly recognized Ike's capitulation for what it was: a purely pragmatic decision to win more votes. But this awareness did not make it any easier for Murrow to swallow: "...Eisenhower couldn't win, presumably, without the Taft boys. But this was Marshall. His Hero. Ike's hero. London. For Chrissake, Marshall had made this man's career."[82]

"He was terribly upset about that speech," said Janet Murrow later. "It was a real betrayal." "I need to tell you that I am sick at heart," wrote New York Times publisher Arthur Sulzberger to Ike's personal campaign manager, Sherman Adams.

Democrats across the country — finding their nominee for president, Adlai Stevenson, running well behind Eisenhower — were uniformly vocal in their criticism of Ike for not publicly denouncing McCarthyism and for betraying Marshall.[83] To Harry S.

---

[80] Presidential Politics. Eisenhower. WGBH American Experience, PBS.
[81] The Fifties, Id., p. 251.
[82] Id.
[83] Joseph McCarthy, The Smithsonian Channel, 12/26/12.

Truman, with his devotion to George Marshall, Eisenhower had committed an act of unpardonable betrayal.[84]

In the end, Ike's charisma and transcendent popularity enabled him to win the November presidential election in a landslide.[85] Despite Stevenson's erudition and wit, he was up against an iconic figure only a relatively short period of time after his greatest triumphs. And Ike's pledge to go to Korea to seek an honorable end to the hostilities if elected, resounded powerfully with the electorate.

All of Ike's jockeying and caution over the McCarthyism issue probably had little impact on the election, one way or the other.

---

[84] <u>Truman</u> by David McCullough (Touchstone, 1992) P. 911.
[85] Eisenhower received 55% of the popular vote and carried 39 states to Stevenson's 8 in the Electoral College.

CHAPTER FOUR

Pretender to the Throne

"McCarthyism is Americanism with its sleeves rolled."
—Joseph R. McCarthy

Joe McCarthy also won re-election to the U.S. Senate handily in the 1952 elections — garnering 54.2% of the vote in Wisconsin.

On the surface, the results on Election Day, November 4, 1952, seemed as big a triumph for McCarthy as for Eisenhower. He had won a decisive victory in his re-election and took a good deal of the credit for driving the Democrats out of the White House while seizing Republican majorities in both the Senate and House of Representatives. And McCarthy felt especially vindicated that he had accomplished all this while rebuffing every effort to repudiate his methods. McCarthy exulted in the heady euphoria of his self-perceived omnipotence.

But, a subtle delusion infected his sense of invincibility. McCarthyism had sustained structural damage barely perceptible to the senses — like a hairline fracture which barely shows up in the x-rays.

Although almost no one knew it at the time, "Eisenhower's election was the beginning of the end" for McCarthy."[86]

On the night of November 4, 1952, as the returns poured in from the elections, "Phil Graham, the publisher of the Washington Post turned to Murray Marder, the Post reporter who had distinguished himself with his intelligent and thorough coverage of the senator [McCarthy] and told him he was going to lose his beat."[87]

Graham was convinced that now that the Republicans had captured the White House, they wouldn't need McCarthy anymore. Though Graham was probably right about that, he was wrong to conclude that what anyone thought at that particular time would diminish the presence and force of Joe McCarthy. Marder grasped this salient point because he knew intimately the degree of McCarthy's recklessness and hatred for authority. Party loyalty did not matter to McCarthy and he didn't care who was in the White House. Marder knew that the McCarthy beat was not finished. In fact, the Post would now need two people to cover it.[88]

In the U.S. Senate, Majority Leader Robert A. Taft, a man of intellect, also now viewed Joseph McCarthy as a loose cannon on the deck. Although it would be foolhardy to oppose him openly, Taft was searching for ways to curb the Wisconsin Republican's power. His first step was to deny the chairmanship of the prestigious Senate Internal Security Committee to McCarthy. Taft's intent was to slow down the McCarthy express.

The appointment went to William Jenner instead.

Taft didn't hold Jenner in any higher esteem than he did McCarthy. But, that was actually the point. Taft knew that Jenner was far less likely to abuse the Internal Security Committee and cause scandal, for the very reason that he was a much smaller personality than McCarthy. Jenner was far less formidable in every category that mattered in politics. He lacked a national following, a strong persona, a highly visible profile and that cult appeal of a McCarthy. McCarthy got his way mostly by instilling fear in his

---

[86] The Fifties, Id., p. 250.
[87] Id.
[88] Id.

potential targets — witness the hammerlock in which he held the Republican national organization — whereas Jenner inspired no such fear. He was both acceptable to the McCarthyites and a safe selection for the leadership.

Like Eisenhower, Phil Graham and many others, Taft underestimated McCarthy's force in America's public life of the early fifties. McCarthy was not brilliant, eloquent or charismatic. And he did not hail from an electoral vote-rich state which would have given him a natural political base. But he had two characteristics that allowed him to wield extraordinary political power for a period of about four and a half years: fearlessness and ruthlessness. Foolish though it may have proved to be in the long-run, during McCarthyism's dynamic, though short run, Joe McCarthy was unafraid to take on anybody, notwithstanding the reputation or clout of the individual. It seemed the bigger they were, the more ruthless and scathing were his attacks. So McCarthy vilified George C. Marshall as being "an evil genius...at the heart of an (anti-American) conspiracy." He renamed Secretary of State Dean Acheson, the "Red Dean" and called Edward R. Murrow a leftist "jackal".

Robert Taft felt a personal obligation to attempt to eviscerate McCarthy's most extreme modus operandi. He wished to atone for empowering McCarthy in 1951 by handing him his first appointments "to the sensitive appropriation bodies,"[89] which had given him his forum. By such appointments, McCarthy had made himself the "Grand Inquisitor"[90] of the State Department. But now, instead of Internal Security, Taft handed McCarthy the Government Operations Committee.

At the time of the appointment, Taft too may have underestimated McCarthy — perhaps due to Taft's failing health — because the Government Operations Committee had a permanent investigations subcommittee which McCarthy quickly turned to his own ends, making himself Chairman and hiring as Chief Counsel a clever twenty-five year old lawyer — an assistant chief prosecutor at

---

[89] Murrow, Id., p. 390.
[90] Id.

the Rosenberg trial — Roy M. Cohn. He also appointed 27 year old Robert F. Kennedy as assistant counsel.

McCarthy was aided in the early days of the Eisenhower Administration by the lack of anyone in official Washington with the stature or inclination to call him out on his actions. Gone from Washington was Harry S. Truman who had once told the press during the Tydings Committee hearings that McCarthy was the "Kremlin's greatest asset in America." The Republican Party now controlled the White House plus both houses of congress. For a significant period in 1953, McCarthy and Cohn were operating in a type of bubble — free from any real criticism or checks and balances. This imbalance, however, would ultimately pave the way for McCarthy's downfall, fortified as it was by his loss of touch with reality.[91]

Notwithstanding such disconnect from reality, however, McCarthy and Cohn took the obscure Investigations Subcommittee and turned it into an offensive weapon. "Running his committee as a personal fiefdom,"[92] McCarthy — with Cohn's invaluable assistance — loudly hunted alleged Communists and "comsymps" in the Voice of America; forced the resignation of the head of the International Information Agency (IIA) and renewed the attack on surviving China experts in the State Department. These were only a few of his aggressive and highly visible initiatives; and with each one McCarthy alienated Eisenhower more and more.

Robert A. Taft, who had been so supportive of McCarthy in his quest for re-election, was also rudely swept aside. When the Senate Majority Leader demanded that McCarthy clear all investigations with him, McCarthy by his actions made it clear that he had no intention of clearing anything with anybody."[93]

In the early months of his administration, Dwight D. Eisenhower felt real constraints upon his ability to publicly oppose McCarthy. He had indorsed McCarthy for re-election only a few months before and in doing so had made him respectable. It would now appear the

---

[91] History of the American People, Id. p. 836.
[92] Murrow, Id. p. 400.
[93] The Fifties, Id., p. 252.

height of hypocrisy and disingenuousness to take him to task before the nation's powerful media.

McCarthy felt no such restraints. No sooner had Eisenhower begun his presidency than McCarthy turned on him. His first attack on Ike was for nominating James B. Conant, the President of Harvard University, as High Commissioner in Germany. This was only the first in a long line of provocative actions taken by McCarthy which seemed designed to undermine Eisenhower, strip away his presidential prerogatives and preempt his position as leader of party and nation.

In his letter to "The President" dated February 3, 1953, Senator McCarthy opened with, "I am strongly opposed to Mr. Conant's confirmation..."[94] He cited four main reasons for his opposition, all of which were based on statements Conant had allegedly made in articles or speeches, copies of which McCarthy did not provide. He did pull selected sentences from offending statements without providing any context. McCarthy offered only his own interpretation of what he alleged was said. In the first instance, he interpreted a Conant speech as advocating the destruction of all industry in Germany, which, said McCarthy, was also advocated in the Morgenthau Plan. According to him, the plan had been largely prepared by accused Communist, Harry Dexter White. Thus, his objection could be boiled down to an interpretation of undisclosed words in a speech that may have resembled undisclosed passages in the Morgenthau Plan, which may have been authored by a man who may have been a subversive. Such guilt by association three or four degrees removed from a perceived Communist threat was quite typical of McCarthyism.

The remaining three grounds for opposing Conant's appointment as High Commissioner of Germany were: McCarthy's assumption that Conant may have been in favor of a high inheritance tax in America; Conant's alleged opposition to Parochial schools; and finally his alleged statement that "there are no Communists at Harvard", which McCarthy claimed may not have been true because

---

[94] The Dwight D. Eisenhower Library, A copy of the McCarthy letter is attached as Appendix B.

although Professors Shapely, Mather and Matthiessen may or may not have been Communists, they espoused what McCarthy claimed were "Communist causes." He provided no other details.

McCarthy's next attack upon Eisenhower came in March of 1953. It turned out to cause a major rift between them. The President nominated State Department veteran, Charles E. Bohlen, to be Ambassador to the Soviet Union. Secretary of State, John Foster Dulles, considered Bohlen to be the most competent man available for the job. Nevertheless, Dulles was not enthusiastic about the nomination. Bohlen had been a minor official at the Yalta Conference in 1945 during the final months of the Roosevelt Administration and of World War II. The Yalta Conference was anathema to Joe McCarthy and many other conservatives. The mere words "Yalta Conference" conjured up for them the specter of appeasement of Joseph Stalin and the Soviet Union. Anyone who attended the conference on behalf of the United States was painted by McCarthy with the same shade of red, regardless of how insignificant a role he had played.

McCarthy tried to defeat the Bohlen nomination from the day Ike announced it. A distressed John Foster Dulles called Bohlen to Foggy Bottom* for a talk. "Couldn't you tell them that you were only an interpreter at Yalta?" Dulles asked the nominee.[95] Dulles went so far as to suggest to Bohlen, whose nickname was "Chip," that on the morning of his appearance before the Senate Confirmation Committee, "they travel in separate cars so that there could be no photographs of them together."[96] At least for that moment, Dulles appeared to have succumbed to the hysteria of McCarthyism. Ike, however, stood firmly behind his appointee. McCarthy then demanded that Dulles, whose duty it was to vouch for Bohlen, testify under oath. Taft responded with fury: "So far as I am concerned Mr. Dulles's statement not under oath is just as good as Mr. Dulles's statement under oath."[97] McCarthy backed down but

---

* Nickname for the State Department headquarters building in Washington, D.C.
[95] The Fifties, Id., p. 252.
[96] Id.
[97] Id.

the damage was done. Both Ike and Taft were livid. As the top two Republican leaders in America, they considered McCarthy to have publicly and boldly broken with his party. When reporters asked Taft after the hearing if he had now broken with McCarthy, he answered "no, no," without any further elaboration. But, in fact he had — and so had Ike.

Taft, with little time left to live, clearly began to distance himself from McCarthy. The latter had not only irretrievably alienated Eisenhower, but had triggered a downward spiral of his influence in the Senate as well. But Taft's fond desire to put McCarthy "where he can't do any harm"[98] had back-fired. Though McCarthy's influence was on the wane, his raw power, which flowed from the pulpit as chairman of the Senate Permanent Subcommittee on Investigations had not. Senator Robert A. Taft died while still in office, on July 31, 1953, from cancer, at the age of 63. His replacement as Majority leader, Senator William F. Knowland of California, was considered by most to be a far lesser man, equipped by neither talent nor inclination to pull back on the reigns of Joe McCarthy. It was now up to Dwight Eisenhower alone — at least within the national government — to curb the power of McCarthy and erase his image from the national landscape.

Though publicly silent, Ike was acutely aware that the McCarthy problem was growing progressively worse. Eisenhower's letter to friend Harry Bullis of May 18, 1953 provides a rare glimpse into his mind-set concerning McCarthy, and into the inner turmoil with which he was beset:[99]

May 18, 1953

Personal and Confidential

Dear Harry:

---

[98] Nightmare in Red: The McCarthy Era in Perspective by Richard M. Fried (Oxford University Press, 1990), p. 134.
[99] Letter Pres. Eisenhower to Harry Bullis, May 18, 1953 Dwight D. Eisenhower Presidential Library and Museum (official File, Box 317, of 99-R, McCarthy). (A copy is attached as Appendix C.)

I emphatically agree with most of what you have to say in your letter of May ninth. I shall certainly take seriously your observation about the Judd case.

With respect to <u>McCarthy</u>, I continue to believe that the President of the United States cannot afford to name names in opposing procedures, practices and methods in our government. This applies with special force when the individual concerned enjoys the immunity of a United States Senator. This particular individual wants, above all else, publicity. Nothing would probably please him more than to get the publicity that would be generated by public repudiation by the President.

I do not mean that there is no possibility that I shall ever change my mind on this point. I merely mean that as of this moment, I consider that the wisest course of action is to continue to pursue a steady, positive policy in foreign relations, in legal procedures in cleaning out the insecure and the disloyal, and in all other areas where McCarthy seems to take such a specific and personal interest. My friends on the Hill tell me that of course, among other things, he wants to increase his appeal as an after-dinner speaker and so raise the fees that he charges.

<u>Personal and Confidential</u>

Mr. Bullis — 2.

It is a sorry mess; at times one feels almost like hanging his head in shame when he reads some of the unreasoned, vicious outbursts of demagoguery that appear in our public prints. But whether a Presidential "crack down" would better, or would actually worsen, the situation, is a moot question.

With all the best,

As ever,

<u>Personal and Confidential</u>

Mr. Harry Bullis,

General Mills Incorporated,

400 Second Avenue South,
Minneapolis 1, Minnesota.

The Bullis letter was a remarkable document of great historical value. The anguish felt by the reserved and tightly controlled Eisenhower could be found in both the words he wrote and between the lines. Such a frank expression of how he really felt about the situation would have surprised no one had it come from Harry Truman. But from the tightly buttoned down Eisenhower it was a rarity. The first three paragraphs of the letter were typical of the reasoned restraint with which he normally operated. But in the revealing last full paragraph, Ike let his emotions flow onto the page in a burst of anger, disgust and sorrow.

As far as the bigger picture was concerned, the Bullis letter expressed several distinct but reconcilable features of Eisenhower's approach to McCarthy. First, whatever he did would be grounded in deeply felt notions of right and wrong. Second, the best course of action for the time being was to not give McCarthy undue publicity, but to give him just enough rope to hang himself. Finally, should this not work, he was prepared to eventually issue a presidential repudiation of McCarthy and all that he stood for.

Ike reprised the same themes in his letter to friend Swede Hazlett, of July 21, 1953[100]; a portion of which addressed the dangers of giving too much publicity to demagogues:

> "...it is quite clear that whenever the President takes part in a newspaper trial of some individual (i.e. referred to earlier in letter as "McCarthy") of whom he disapproves, one thing is automatically accomplished. This is an increase in the headline value of the individual attacked. I think that the average honorable individual cannot understand to what lengths certain politicians would go for publicity. They

---

[100] DDE's Papers as President, Name Series, Box 18, Dwight D. Eisenhower Presidential Library and Museum.

have learned a simple truth in American life. This is that the most vicious kind of attack from one element always creates a very great popularity, amounting to almost hero worship, in an opposite fringe of society."

After citing the example of Huey Long and his idolaters, Eisenhower expanded upon his theme:

"When you have a situation like this, you have an ideal one for newspapers, the television and the radio to exploit, to exaggerate and to perpetuate. In such a situation I disagree completely with the 'crackdown theory'. I believe in the positive approach. I believe that we should earnestly support the practice of American principles in trials and investigations — we should teach and preach decency and justice. We should support — even militantly support — people whom we know to be unjustly attacked, whether they are public servants or private citizens...the indirect defense accomplished through condemnation of unfair methods is always applicable.

Persistence in these unspectacular but sound methods will, in my opinion, produce results that may not be headlines but they will be permanent because they will earn the respect of fair-minded citizens — which means the vast bulk of our population."

Eisenhower went on to reject succumbing to anger or irritation in the McCarthy situation, which could result in an ill-advised outburst. He clearly favored the patient approach, which he emphatically articulated again in his letter to his brother, Dr. Milton Eisenhower of October 9, 1953:

"As for McCarthy. Only a short-sighted or completely inexperienced individual would urge the use of the office of the Presidency to give an opponent the publicity he so avidly desires. Time and again... ... have stood for the right of the individual for free expression of convictions even though those convictions might be unpopular, and for uncensored use of our libraries, except as dictated by common decency...

Permit me to say that I think there would be far more progress made against so-called 'McCarthy'-ism if individuals of an opposing purpose would take it upon themselves to help sustain and promote their own ideals, rather than to wait and wait for a blasting of their pet enemies by someone else... I have no intention whatsoever of helping to promote the publicity value of anyone who disagrees with me — demagogue or not..."[101]

The Bullis, Hazlett and Milton Eisenhower letters leave no room to doubt that Ike had, during his early presidency, promulgated and consistently carried out a steadfast policy on Joe McCarthy — one of stoic patience rather than public confrontation.

The intriguing question remains, however, whether he really believed in his heart of hearts that his policy was going to work. Ike's vast experience in dealing with difficult and stubborn men surely must have told him that some hyper-aggressive personalities never check or temper their aggressiveness. Confronted with adversaries who employ passive and patient resistance, they invariably become even more aggressive. Undoubtedly, Ike had factored this into his strategy, by concluding that passive resistance would eventually cause McCarthy to self-destruct. He got the self-

[101] DDE's Papers as President, Name Series, Box 12, Eisenhower Milton 1952-53, Dwight D. Eisenhower Presidential Library and Museum.

destruct part right, but a strong case could be made that only a vigorous counter attack upon McCarthy in open view of the whole world would be sufficient to bring him down.

Certainly as the color of the leaves in the greenery along the banks of the Potomac reached the height of their beauty — vivid amber, red and orange colors — and Washington was beginning its wind-down to a special Thanksgiving Holiday on which America could celebrate the return of its sons from the Korean War, one public figure was anything but grateful for America's bounty.

In a speech on the Senate floor Joseph R. McCarthy gave vent to a bitter diatribe, the central theme of which he expressed with thinly-veiled anger, as follows:

> "You are seeing today an all-out attempt to marshal the forces of the opposition using not merely the Communists, or their fellow travelers — the deluded liberals, the egg heads and some of my good friends in both the Democratic and Republican Parties who can become heroes overnight in the eyes of the left-wing press if they will just join with the Jackal pack."

This was a mere prelude to what was to come next.

CHAPTER FIVE

Escalation of Hostilities

On Tuesday evening, November 24, 1953, McCarthy went on nationwide radio and television to lambast his perceived adversaries in a fiery and provocative address. McCarthy began graciously enough by praising the Eisenhower Administration for removing "1,456 Truman holdovers who were...gotten rid of because of Communist connections and activities or perversion."[102] But in a sudden and dramatic change of tone he accused the Administration of still having on its payroll after eleven months, John Paton Davies, Jr., an alleged leftist. Not uncommonly, McCarthy was wrong on his facts because Davies had been dismissed three weeks earlier. Even worse, he then repeated the unsubstantiated allegation he had raised many times before, that Davies had tried to "put Communists and espionage agents in key spots in the Central Intelligence Agency."[103] But McCarthy was just warming up. He next accused Eisenhower of

---

[102] McCarthyism, The Great American Scare: A Documentary History by Albert Fried (Oxford University Press, 1997) pp. 182-184.
[103] Id.

not doing enough to secure the release of missing American pilots shot down over China in the Korean War.[104]

C.D. Jackson, a speechwriter and Special Assistant to the President, summed up what was becoming the prevailing view of McCarthy in the White House in the following pithy and blunt portion of his official notes of Friday, November 27, 1953:[105]

> "Tuesday night McCarthy made sensational radio and television talk. My impression was aside from open season on lambasting Truman, that McCarthy had (a) declared war on Eisenhower; (b) by subtle innuendo had accused Truman of; (c) had attempted to establish McCarthy as Mr. Republican; (d) had attempted to establish McCarthyism as Republicanism, and anybody who didn't agree was either a fool or a protector of Communism."

Jackson then went on to highlight the absurdity of the type of logic often employed by the McCarthyites:

> "Wonderful syllogism — I am the only effective rooter-outer of Communists; there are still Communists in Government (Davies); this Government headed by Eisenhower; therefore unless Eisenhower roots them out my way, he is a harborer of Communists."[106]

In confirmation of Jackson's take on the situation, he wrote: "James Reston (syndicated columnist for the New York Times*....

---

[104] Id.
[105] C.D. Jackson Papers, Box 68, Log 1953 (3), Dwight D. Eisenhower Presidential Library and Museum.
[106] Ibid.
* Information in parenthesis added by author.

asked me personally what I thought and I replied that I thought McCarthy had declared war on the President."[107]

Responding to flack that he was getting from other White House staffers for his bluntness about McCarthy, Jackson wrote trenchantly — but even more bluntly — the following:[108]

> "...Consider it disastrous appeasement which began September 1952, when the campaign train crossed Wisconsin border and the boys persuaded Eisenhower to take out reference to General Marshall in his Milwaukee speech; that was the beginning."[109]

The White House staff meeting held on November 30, 1953 (referred to by Jackson as "Black Monday") was rife with heated disagreements over McCarthy.[110] Staffers Jerry Morgan, Homer Greunther and Jack Martin jumped on Jackson for having said to journalist James Reston that McCarthy had declared war on the President. And Press Secretary James Hagerty "cautioned against talking, saying that it inevitably was embarrassing to the President." Hagerty, however, "was very low pitch and temperate about [sic, the] whole thing." Only two of the men present at the meeting, Willis and Harlow, spoke up for Jackson, who described the meeting as a "big rhubarb".

In his own defense, Jackson forthrightly warned all those present that the "Three Little Monkeys Act was not working and would not work, and that appeasing McCarthy to save his 7 votes for this year's legislative program was poor tactics, poor strategy and poor arithmetic, and that unless the President stepped up to bat on this one soon, the Republicans would have neither a program nor 1954, nor 1956."[111] After Jackson spoke so forcefully, any further criticism of his position was muted.

---

[107] Ibid.
[108] Ibid.
[109] Ibid.
[110] Notes from the day by C. D. Jackson, (C.D. Jackson Papers, Box 68, Log 1953 (5)), Dwight D. Eisenhower Presidential Library and Museum.
[111] Ibid.

C.D. Jackson had, however, opened Pandora's box. Two days later an intra-staff memo written by Stanley M. Rumbough, Jr. and Charles Masterson[112] sought to consolidate the disparate positions among White House insiders in favor of a presidential response to McCarthy, into one integrated statement. Among the key points made in the memo were:

> *A. The image of the President as an inspirational leader to the independent voter must be preserved.*
>
> *B. The threat to the president's legislative program by his speaking out against McCarthyism is questionable; and there is no assurance any way that appeasement of McCarthyism would help the program;*
>
> *C. People are swayed by emotion more than reason and this is an emotional issue;*
>
> *D. The image of the President as a fighter may well be more important politically than the success or failure of his legislative program;*
>
> *E. One of the most dramatic moments in the President's career has arrived. He can appeal to the people now as a popular leader who has been attacked;*
>
> *F. Furthermore, in speaking out against McCarthyism he is on the side of the angels.*

The suggested course of action urged in the memo was:

> *A. Schedule a press conference in which Ike can field questions on McCarthy;*
>
> *B. Have Dulles answer specific McCarthy charges re: Davies;*
>
> *C. Include in press conference an opening statement asserting the proud record of the President in fighting Communism. But state that in continuing this fight the Administration shall not abandon the concept of fair play.*

---

[112] Memorandum, Stanley M. Rumbough, Jr. and Charles Masterson to Murray Snyder, Assistant White House Press Secretary, dated 12/1/53 (Box 68, McCarthy) (Attached as Appendix F).

On Wednesday, December 2, 1953, the same staffers who had engaged in the discussions of "Black Monday" trooped into the President's office with a proposed statement prepared as a follow-up to the intra-staff memo of December 1st.

The statement was handed to the President who read it quickly and with obvious irritation. He made some "mumbling" critical comments as he read.[113] Staff Member Jack Martin spoke first: "Mr. President, a vacuum exists in this country, and it is a political vacuum. Unless you sir, fill it in, somebody else will." The President twisted and squirmed, a sign of his discomfort with what Martin had just said. The latter stood his ground. Stirred by Martin's courage, C. D. Jackson was next to speak: "Mr. President, so long as Taft was alive, you were able to defer to him in leading the party. But now you can no longer avoid the responsibility of leadership. People are waiting for a sign, a simple sign, and now is the time."

Jackson then handed the President and all others present a copy of his proposed statement for the press conference. This triggered a contentious exchange among the meeting participants over the text of the statement.

The President had read Jackson's statement with even greater irritation. Slamming it back at Jackson, he spoke angrily: "I will not refer to McCarthy personally. I will not get into the gutter with that guy."

But the discussion was gathering steam and momentum and as it continued, Eisenhower's mood began to change. He picked up the original statement and re-read it — this time more slowly and carefully. He himself began to suggest revisions to the text.

Then everyone's mood began to change. The snarling gave way to constructive suggestions to help the president as they worked in harmony. Finally, Eisenhower took the reins completely and in a demonstration of real leadership, dictated the last paragraph as it finally appeared. What had begun in Jackson's words as a "ghastly mess" ended well.

---

[113] Notes from the day of C.D. Jackson, December 2, 1953 [C.D. Jackson Papers, Box 68, Log 1953 (8)].

Jackson's final comment in his notes, however, revealed anxiety over the path ahead: "Problem now is, having zippered the toga of Republican political leadership on the President's shoulders, how to keep that zipper shut."[114]

Senator Joseph R. McCarthy (19081957), ca. 1954
National Archives and Records Administration

Dwight Eisenhower had a very different leadership style than some of his advisers. He was known "as a harmonizer, a man who could get diverse factions to work toward a common goal...leadership he explained meant patience and conciliation, not hitting people over the head."[115] But, Joseph McCarthy was not interested in conciliation. The goals he fervently pursued — to be the leader of the Republican Party, the most powerful politician in the nation and, perhaps, eventually President of the United States —

[114] Ibid.
[115] McCarthyism, The Great American Red Scare by Albert Fried, Ibid. pp. 182-184 (Oxford University Press, 1997).

could not be conciliated. Anything short of hitting him over the head appeared to be a feckless technique for dissuading him from the all-out pursuit of those goals. Before the end of 1953, McCarthy disabused the theretofore unconvinced advisers to the President of the notion that he had not declared war on the Eisenhower presidency.

Always vocal and scathing in his accusations against the Truman and Roosevelt Administrations, of "twenty years of treason," McCarthy had now shockingly tarred the Eisenhower Administration with the same brush. He had modified his condemnation to "21 years of treason" so as to include the first year of the Eisenhower Administration.

As the old year gave way to the new, it was clear that in order to battle McCarthyism, the country needed the Ike of 1945, who had faced down the German generals and told them face to face that he would accept no terms other than unconditional surrender. The intriguing question on the minds and lips of the Eisenhower people as the year 1954 began was whether an America polarized over the methods of Joe McCarthy would support the President in his efforts. Without strong presidential leadership in exposing McCarthy and his methods for what they were, it seemed highly doubtful.

CHAPTER SIX

McCarthy on the Attack

History rarely reveals itself while it is happening. Although historians often refer to the election of Dwight D. Eisenhower as the beginning of the end for Joe McCarthy, that judgment emanates from the wisdom of hindsight and was clearly not evident on January 1, 1954. As the new year began, McCarthy seemed to be gathering, not losing, steam and was on the attack on several fronts.

The question most commonly asked by Americans to each other in 1953-54 was, "Are you pro or con?" It wasn't even necessary to identify the unstated "what" in the question. Those who would ask or answer the question knew that the silent "what" was McCarthy. The larger penetrating and polarizing questions floating above the nation's consciousness were: How far is it permissible to go in fighting domestic communism; and, How big a price were Americans willing to pay in loss of personal liberties, dignity and decency?

Today's polarization in America over issues like gun control, gay marriage, immigration and abortion have a clear parallel in the divide over McCarthy and his methods in the early nineteen fifties.

McCarthy-induced polarization was, however, unique. The hot-button issues in 2014 are similarly laden with highly emotional content; but present significant differences in intensity.

For one thing the "24/7" news cycle of today is breath — taking in the speed and breadth with which it bombards the viewing and listening public. But the needs of the purveyors of both electronic and print news, caused by a highly competitive market, compel them to quickly move on to the next hot story, often within days and sometimes hours. This lightning-quick penetration of the national psyche by the news media, followed by an equally rapid withdrawal of an issue from meaningful attention, has had a psychological impact on the news-consuming public. Over-exposure to news stories has eroded their quality and significance in the minds of millions across the globe. It has also shortened attention spans and patience. Add to this the large number of controversial issues with which the public is involved or exposed, and the issues become diffuse, with each individual subject diminished in intensity. The news-consuming public in America clearly suffers from media over-exposure with news stories requiring a high concentration level often beyond its capacity to assimilate. And the desultory treatment of complex subjects by the media often has the effect of trivializing them.

In 1950 through 1954, however, there was only one transcendent issue and that was McCarthyism. Unless one were comatose during that time span it is hard to imagine his or her not having heard of Joseph McCarthy. The issues permeating the culture of 2014 are intense, and the nationwide polarization concerning them is real. But still, each of the hot-button issues of today resonates most urgently with a particular interest group. McCarthyism and its hand-maiden, militant anti-communism, resonated with a large majority of Americans on a fundamental gut-level. Embraced within the narrow, micro-issue of whether one was "pro or con" McCarthy, were the macro-issues: What constituted a good American? How far was it permissible for a society to go in attempting to protect itself from its enemies? and, Which human rights and civil liberties contained within the concept of Americanism were so essential to its identity, that they must never be sacrificed? Intersecting these abstract questions were concrete events — world-wide Soviet aggression, the Iron Curtain, the American spy trials, the globalization of the nuclear threat and the Korean War. All of this produced a combustible brew.

The polarization wrought by the divisiveness of McCarthyism had superseded political parties and traditional institutions by the spring of 1954. Republican Joseph McCarthy, an Irish-Catholic, had the unwavering support of the Kennedys of Massachusetts and their patriarch, Joseph P. Kennedy, staunch Democrats all.

On the other hand, McCarthy was on the outs with many members of his own party — most significantly in the Republican administration of Dwight D. Eisenhower; and with the President himself.

Even traditionally conservative institutions such as the Protestant Churches of America, the U.S. Army and the CIA had felt the sting of McCarthy's attacks and had largely turned against him. On the other hand, he enjoyed strong and vocal support from the pulpits of the Catholic churches in America.

In Congress McCarthy could count on strong support from conservative Republicans — particularly in the midwest and west — but had lost the support of most moderate Republicans in the Eastern states.

The nationwide dissonance over McCarthyism was also peculiarly personal. Even the national divide over slavery in the 1850's and 1860's made allowances for geographical differences.

With McCarthyism, however, geography was not a major factor in its personalization. The geography might include the next house over, the adjoining bar stool or the next lane in the bowling alley. And McCarthyism by its nature was highly personal in its accusations and attacks. One can have "differing views today on gay rights, gun control or immigration reform without necessarily being vilified. More often than not, in the early 50's, if the individual in the house next door, the adjoining church pew or the next seat over on the commuter train, was critical of McCarthy's positions or methods, he often was loudly and publicly accused of being a "pinko", a "fellow traveler" or a "comsymp". Such openly hostile, ad hominem attacks, could and often did damage the accused persons in the eyes of their neighbors, friends, relatives, co-workers and employers.

Thus, the pervasive environment of fear in America transcended geography and status. It extended from the highest levels of government, industry and the professions to the back-yard barbecue or neighborhood bridge game — and every level in between. Its by-products included loss of careers, jobs, reputations, standing in the community, friends, neighbors and close family relationships. It had a devastatingly chilling effect upon the constitutional rights of free speech, assembly, free press and due process of law, among others. No estrangement between Americans of differing views was as pronounced and bitter, save for the rending of the Union in the Civil War.

President Dwight D. Eisenhower was absolutely appalled by the rending of the fabric of America caused by McCarthyism; but was ambivalent over how best to combat it. Cataclysmic events in the year 1954 would prove to force his hand.

In the meantime, Joseph McCarthy sought to solidify his power base by making speeches designed to coalesce the two groups upon whose support he chiefly relied: political conservatives and American Catholics. Typical of his efforts was the following shrewdly worded excerpt from one of his major addresses:

> "The fate of the world rests with the atheism of Moscow and the Christian spirit throughout other parts of the world."

On this and many other occasions McCarthy coupled Catholic anti-communism with the use of anti-communism as a key part of the Cold War with the Soviet Union. Hence, McCarthy sought to portray his activism as not only necessary to the survival of the free world, but sanctioned by God. In his mind's eye he was God's nominated representative on Earth for combating Godless Communism. He was anointed to lead and organize the crusade.

After linking the Eisenhower Administration to the alleged treason of its predecessor, in late 1953, McCarthy used his permanent Subcommittee on Investigations to launch a probe of communist influence in the Voice of America. The Voice of

America was then administered by the United States Information Agency, a subdivision of the U.S. Department of State.

Hearings of McCarthy's Subcommittee on Investigations were held. Voice of America personnel were subpoenaed to appear and be interrogated in front of TV cameras and packed press galleries. Like a hostile defense counsel cross-examining a key prosecution witness, McCarthy laced into each witness with leading questions loaded with innuendo and insinuations.[116] The Q & A did produce some allegations of communist influence on the content of broadcasts. But, they went no further than the accusation stage for want of any semblance of substantiation. As Ike seethed in silence, morale at the Voice of America plummeted to an all-time low. One of its engineers even committed suicide during McCarthy's probe.

One of the policy advisors for the Voice of America, Edward Kretzman, in his retrospective of the investigation, commented that it was VOA's "darkest hour when Senator McCarthy and his chief hatchet man, Roy Cohn, almost succeeded in muffling it."[117]

McCarthy's goal in the VOA probe was to unearth treason in the Voice of America. Like most of his anti-communist campaigns, this one was long on sensationalism and short on results.

Although it was not clear whether it was McCarthy's idea or Roy Cohn's, the committee shifted its sights away from the formidable burden of proof required of its attack on the VOA, to a phase of the USIA's* operations presenting a fatter target, the USIA's oversees libraries. The decision was made that Roy Cohn would embark upon a highly publicized trip to Western Europe with his friend, the handsome G. David Schine, in tow as his aide and travelling companion. Once in Europe, they were to investigate the USIA libraries. They traipsed across Western Europe, staying at the best hotels, and staging surprise raids on multiple libraries, in their quest to identify pro-communist or other subversive publications. They would then report their findings to McCarthy, who would demand the removal of the publications.

---

[116] Voice of America, A History, by Alan L. Heil, Columbia University Press, 2003, p. 53.
[117] Id.
* United States Information Agency.

Cohn and Schine, unlike in the VOA-personnel investigation, didn't have to prove or substantiate anything. All they had to do was declare books to be un-American, add them to the list and provide the list to McCarthy. McCarthy would then demand that the State Department order their removal from the library shelves.

The decision to list the books was based solely on the opinions of Cohn and Schine. They served as constables, prosecutors, judge and jury as to the fate of the books; and their decisions were immune from appeal. They were censors, reportable and answerable to no one. And neither man was much past 25 years of age.

For the two young, yet well connected men, the book-banning crusade was a several week all-expenses paid, European junket at taxpayer expense. They did not even view the offending books. All they had to do was check the library card catalog for supposedly pro-communist authors. McCarthy picked it up from there, reciting the list of objectionable authors before the Investigations Subcommittee and the news media.

The Department of State, in a shamefully pusillanimous act, bowed to McCarthy and ordered its overseas librarians to remove from their shelves "material by any controversial persons, Communists, fellow travelers, etc." Shockingly, some of the overseas librarians burned the newly-forbidden books.[118]

The book banning and burning did not escape Eisenhower's attention. He was so incensed by it that during a speech at Dartmouth College in Hanover, New Hampshire, he railed against the campaign in blunt and powerful words: "Don't join the book burners," said Ike. "Don't think you are going to conceal faults by concealing evidence that they ever existed. Don't be afraid to go to your library and read every book."[119]

Not a single well-informed person is known to have had any doubt that Ike had aimed his barbed comments straight at Joe McCarthy. Eisenhower was hardly a day-to-day champion of civil liberties. But he was highly intelligent and hated what he believed

---

[118] The Politics of Fear: Joseph R. McCarthy and The Senate, by Robert Griffith, University of Mass Press, p. 216.
[119] Ike, An American Hero, Id., p. 673.

was anti-democratic suppression of freedom of expression. He had a particular enmity for suppression of creative products of the written word. He had no fancy rationale for his ideas about freedom and liberty. To him they were just what fairness and good sense required. And speaking out as he did at Dartmouth required no small amount of courage. Starkly implicit in the words Eisenhower spoke was a disavowal of the capitulation by his own valued Secretary of State, John Foster Dulles, to McCarthy's demands. The State Department had actually pledged cooperation with the hearings concerning the Voice of America and the U.S.I.A. libraries. "Foreign Service personnel," reported Edward R. Murrow, were "scared to death...afraid of Senator McCarthy and the Committee Staff."[120]

Murrow further opined that, "so far as Senator McCarthy's investigations are concerned, the record merely indicates that neither President Eisenhower nor Secretary Dulles are prepared to criticize or condemn either his objectives or his tactics."

Murrow was clearly correct about Dulles. Eisenhower's posture as to McCarthy, however, was more layered and nuanced. The President was consistent throughout his administration in not criticizing individuals by name — considering such personalization to be unseemly and inappropriate for a chief executive. He believed it to be beneath the dignity of the office. Ike had no qualms, however, about leveling serious criticism at McCarthy. One need only read between the lines and fill in the blanks to gather his obvious meaning.

A clear pattern was emerging. McCarthy would attack the Administration's nominees for official posts or those already in government, while using his committee to seek to uncover treason in Administration programs, departments and agencies. Each time he attacked, Ike would vigorously, albeit obliquely, defend his administration, but without mentioning McCarthy by name. McCarthy's increase in his allegation of 20 years of treason" to "21 years of treason" had created a state of war between Ike and

---

[120] Murrow, Id., p. 401.

McCarthy. But, as of early March, 1954, Eisenhower had not yet launched a counter-offensive. It soon would come.

In the meantime, McCarthy's offensive escalated, prompting Adlai Stevenson, while addressing Southeastern Democrats on March 6, 1954, to charge over TV and radio that "a political party divided against itself, half McCarthy and half Eisenhower, could not produce national unity..."[121]

The skirmishes continued with parry and thrust. Upon his appointment as Chairman of the Investigations Subcommittee, McCarthy had appointed Joseph Brown Matthews (known as J.B. Matthews) as the subcommittee's staff director. Matthews had previously been a research director of the House Committee on Un-American activities (HUAC). In some circles, he was regarded as one of the nation's foremost anti-communists. In others he was simply known as McCarthy's "hit man".

Controversy arose with the suddenness of a flash tornado when it was learned that Matthews had written an article entitled "Reds and our Churches".[122] The opening sentence of the article was, "The largest single group supporting the communist apparatus in the United States is composed of 'Protestant Clergymen'." He further charged in the article that at least seven thousand Protestant clergymen had served "the Kremlin conspiracy...supporting the Communist apparatus in the U.S...."[123] This was a staggering accusation, immediately bringing cries of protest across the nation. A bipartisan group in the U.S. Senate — McCarthy's colleagues — denounced this "shocking and unwarranted attack against the American Clergy." They coupled their denunciation with a demand that McCarthy fire Matthews. As the controversy grew, a majority of McCarthy's own committee joined the call for Matthews' ouster.

At the White House, the President — like all presidents up to that time — was a Protestant himself. He was not going to let Matthews' statements go unchallenged. With no attempt to keep it confidential, Eisenhower fired off a telegram of support to an ecumenical group

---

[121] <u>Murrow</u>, Id., p. 430.
[122] Often misidentified as "Reds In Our Churches".
[123] <u>Ike</u>, Id., p. 673.

protesting the attack on the clergy. The telegram created a "sensation" as once again Ike had rebuked McCarthy without stating his name.[124] McCarthy was besieged from all quarters.

After stubbornly refusing to dismiss Matthews for several weeks, McCarthy finally yielded to the pressure and accepted Matthews's resignation. McCarthy's opponents took great encouragement from his retreat on the Matthews controversy, seeing it as a clear sign that he was not invincible.[125] For once, he had been forced to back down.

Ike's tactic of calling out McCarthy without naming him was working.

Undaunted, however, McCarthy remained in attack mode. By wielding his power in Congress he accelerated the process of "blacklisting." Blacklisting dated as far back as November 1947 when at a meeting of Hollywood producers, a list was drawn up of names of alleged Communists working in the movie business. Under pressure from HUAC and anti-communist groups, the producers created the "blacklist" to discourage the entertainment industry from employing the persons whose names appeared on the list. For the producers it was an act of self-preservation combined with desperation.

Between 1951 and 1954 the House Committee on Un-American Activities — then under the powerful influence of McCarthy — "named 324 Hollywood personalities, who were thereafter blacklisted."[126] As a presidential candidate, Dwight D. Eisenhower, had written to the chairman of HUAC after meeting with the committee, stating his opposition to the listing and dissemination of names of persons accused of anti-American activities. He stated clearly and forcefully in his letter that he considered the publication of names of those merely accused of being Communists, a violation of their civil liberties and right to due process of law. The letter was buried and never appeared in the Congressional Record.

Many of the blacklisted individuals, most of whom were neither indicted for, nor convicted of, any crime, such as actor John

[124] Ike, Id., p. 673.
[125] The Politics of Fear, Joseph R. McCarthy and the Senate, Id., p. 233.
[126] History of the American People, Id., p. 835.

Garfield, never worked again in the entertainment industry. Their names had been sullied, reputations destroyed and chosen careers in tatters. Some of the bigger names such as Arthur Miller and Zero Mostel had enough resiliency to make comebacks after McCarthy's influence and that of HUAC began to wane. A number of Hollywood screen writers managed to stay afloat through the use of paid "fronts", who lent their names as the supposed writers of scripts and publications, actually written by blacklisted writers, forced to remain anonymous.

"The winter of 1953-54, observed Edward R. Murrow, "would be remembered by many as the depths of the McCarthy Era, turning at times into a theater of the absurd." During those months an Indiana text book commissioner declared Robin Hood a Communist because of his reputed practice of taking from the rich to give to the poor.

Also recommended during those winter months was a purge and redaction of all text book references to the Society of Friends, upon the grounds that Quakers did not believe in fighting wars.

McCarthyesque statements and actions had become scripts in a theater of the absurd, peopled by a cast of minions from coast to coast, with Joe McCarthy as producer — director and Roy Cohn as assistant director.

By the winter of 1954, McCarthy was beginning to run out of new high-profile targets to lock within his cross-hairs. Despite the fact that large segments of the population still equated the demand for civil liberties with subversion, McCarthy's theretofore enormous popularity was beginning to fray at the edges. Of course, anyone as big as McCarthy was not going to plummet in popularity all at once. His decline was, at that juncture, an erosion rather than an implosion.

While probably desperate to make a big media splash comparable to those created by "205 Communists in the State Department" and "20 years of treason", McCarthy took a huge misstep by opening fire on the CIA, accusing the huge federal spy agency of being infiltrated by Communist subversives.

McCarthy's Achilles Heel had always been his lack of evidence to back up his charges. With the CIA it was doubly so. His growing desperation, combined with his heavy drinking, was clouding his judgment. McCarthyism worked most effectively when its individual or group target was already shrouded under suspicion, such as Owen Lattimore, Harry Dexter White and the Department of State of Franklin D. Roosevelt. But he couldn't have picked a worse objective than the CIA. One of the most opaque — least transparent — agencies in the world, the CIA was a problematic target. Attacking the CIA was like trying to attack fog. All the CIA had to do was issue a denial of all accusations. No one could prove otherwise because their operations were secret. If by chance, a particular accusation hit a nerve, the CIA's public information reps would simply refuse to discuss the matter because it was classified. And with virtually no effective oversight, the agency was mostly immune from accountability. The informed public and Washington insiders knew and accepted this about the CIA. When McCarthy attacked the agency, America — for the most part — shrugged.

McCarthy, having been rebuffed and ignored, upped the ante by officially calling for a Congressional investigation of Communists and Comsymps in the CIA. In doing so, he escalated his war with the White House to a new level. Ike and his deputies immediately hunkered down to block the investigation.

On June 8, 1954, the President met with top advisers Adams, Persons, Hagerty, Snyder, Montgomery, Harlow and Morgan. "McCarthy's threat to Investigate the CIA" was one of the major items on the agenda. Eisenhower took the lead. He informed his advisers that he was going to call a bi-partisan meeting of the Congressional leaders and "present to them the reasons why it is impossible for any individual or group outside of the administrative branch to investigate our intelligence organization."[127]

The President deflected McCarthy's call for a Congressional investigation. At a luncheon and meeting he told his advisory group that since McCarthy had charged that the CIA was riddled with Communists, he intended to appoint a Presidential Commission to look into the charges. Those present at the luncheon were to

---

[127] Diary entry by James Hagerty, White House Press Secretary [James C. Hagerty Papers, Box 1, June 1954] Dwight D. Eisenhower Library and Museum.

emphasize that the country could have no Intelligence if our programs were constantly subjected to investigation by members of Congress. The bi-partisan meeting was to be held on the following Monday, June 14th. At the meeting Ike would produce a letter to the President from the head of the CIA, Allen Dulles, strongly citing the reasons for refusing to cooperate with a Congressional investigation. Ike displayed confidence that he would receive one hundred percent support from both the Democrat and Republican Congressional leaders. Ike wanted the bi-partisan meeting to signal opposition to McCarthy from the entire leadership of Congress.

Eisenhower felt so optimistic about his plan that he leaned back in his chair and with a trademark smile on his face, mused pleasurably about the week ahead. First he expressed the hope that McCarthy would "sound off" once again on his threat to investigate the CIA, prior to the scheduled bi-partisan meeting. "My boys, I am convinced of one thing," said the President. "The more we can get McCarthy threatening to investigate our Intelligence, the more public support we are going to get. If there is any way I could trick him into renewing his threat, I would be very happy to do so...and then let him have it."[128]

Ike had reason to be sanguine about the CIA controversy. Senate Republican Majority Leader, Edward F. Knowland, had been in for an off-the-record visit that very morning, together with CIA Director Allen Dulles. The three men had reviewed McCarthy's threat against the CIA. Knowland expressed confidence that he could get bi-partisan support on Capitol Hill against McCarthy.

McCarthy's threat of an investigation died a quiet death. The President, the Congressional leadership and the National Security Council had stood shoulder to shoulder against it — thereby ensuring its doom.

---

[128] Hagerty Diary entry, Id.

CHAPTER SEVEN

Murrow and McCarthy

Although the Winter of 1953-54 saw several instances of successful opposition by President Eisenhower to Senator McCarthy's attacks on presidential appointees, the V.O.A., the U.S.I.A., the Protestant Churches and the CIA, McCarthy's popularity in early 1954 was still high. Substantial majorities of Americans queried in Gallop Polls expressed approval of McCarthy and his investigations. The polling particularly revealed that anti-communism was a powerful political issue; one that McCarthy intended to introduce into the 1954 Congressional elections , at the same time the Eisenhower Administration was repeatedly declaring it to be a non-issue.

With the wisdom of hindsight, one can see that McCarthy was planting the seeds of his own destruction in the winter of '54, a process which was then not evident to most.

Still in awe of McCarthy's power and influence, most members of the news media and political establishment were unwilling to take McCarthy on in any kind of direct confrontation. One exception was famed World War II foreign correspondent and TV journalist, Edward R. Murrow.

Murrow always had a rare intuitiveness as to the news-worthiness and potential controversy engendered in events others dismissed as mundane. Thus, when McCarthy hauled Brigadier General Ralph W. Zwicker before his committee to answer for the promotion and honorable discharge he had granted to Army dentist, Irving Peress — after the latter took the Fifth concerning his political affiliations — Murrow knew instinctively that McCarthy was playing with dynamite. After all, a former general sat in the White House. Then when McCarthy went on to abuse General Zwicker, a decorated war hero, as having the intelligence of a "five-year-old child" and one who was "not fit to wear that uniform," Murrow knew immediately that McCarthy had made a dangerous misstep that would come back to haunt him. What very few journalists and politicians knew on February 18, 1954, the day McCarthy made his incendiary remarks, was that the time was then ripe to expose McCarthy for what he was.

Murrow and his "See It Now" producer, Fred Friendly, were exceptions to the general rule that McCarthy was immune from criticism. They saw with sharp, clarity that their employer, CBS News, could reap a windfall of favorable attention by devoting a half-hour TV show to an exposé of Joseph R. McCarthy. They also considered McCarthy to present a grave danger to civil liberties and that his exposure was long overdue.

The two weeks leading up to Murrow's fateful segment of "See It Now" were marked by the ebb and flow of a type of point-counterpoint interaction between the Eisenhower Administration and McCarthy. The Administration's opening salvo was a bold move by Army Secretary Robert Ten Broeck Stevens in publicly refusing to allow any further testimony by General Zwicker before the McCarthy Committee. But then in an attempt to defuse the state of open hostility between McCarthy and the Department of the Army, Secretary Stevens agreed to meet with McCarthy and several top Republicans for a peace-making luncheon. The luncheon had been orchestrated by the White House; and Stevens acted out his part as conciliator, while making significant concessions to McCarthy and appearing to capitulate to his demands.

The participants were said to have dined on southern fried chicken, an unfortunate menu choice for the Administration, since it led the press to thereafter refer to the event as "The Chicken Luncheon".

Murrow began furiously reviewing footage of filmed appearances McCarthy had made; and transcripts of the Zwicker hearings, his speeches and press conferences. Murrow worked non-stop at CBS News's offices in Manhattan wearing blue jeans with suspenders and a red hunter's shirt; cutting and splicing sections of film, and editing them to depict only the most powerful and representative words from McCarthy's mouth. Finally, he and his staff interwove the film cuts with Murrow's narrative, in a sometimes frantic effort to produce a coherent and cohesive one-half hour TV show — one which would grab the viewers' attention without resorting to sensationalism, exaggeration or distortion. An exposé of McCarthy would hardly be worth much if it resorted to the same techniques he used. Murrow selected March 9, 1954 as the date of his nationwide broadcast.

Almost as if fate was cooperating in ratcheting up the pre-broadcast publicity and hype, on February 25th — one day after the "Chicken Luncheon" — Stevens told the press he would not accede to the abuse of Army personnel. The dramatic change in tone from his posture a little more than twenty four hours earlier, led to the almost inescapable conclusion that he was speaking on orders from his boss, the President of the United States. Confirmation of this surmise came from White House Press Secretary, James Hagerty, who told the press that Eisenhower had endorsed Stevens's tough statement.

The bold position taken by Secretary Stevens touched off "what newsroom memos were calling 'the hottest political story in years', a red-hot intraparty fight."[129] Hagerty's diary entry concerning the controversy was a succinct, "Everybody's jittery."[130]

Following daily events closely, Murrow called his staff together and gave them a two word order concerning the scheduled March 9,

---

[129] Murrow, Id., p. 429.
[130] James Hagerty Diary Entry, February 25, 1954.

1954 "See It Now" broadcast: "We go!"[131] In an unprecedented action reflecting Murrow's unique status, CBS President, William Paley, granted Murrow carte blanche in the preparation of the McCarthy exposé. The show would go on the air with the CBS hierarchy wholly ignorant of its content. Of course, that also gave the top executives plausible denial.

On the Sunday before the show was scheduled to air, nervous tension pervaded the "See It Now" offices. The entire staff was on edge. "The terror is right here in this room," said Murrow.[132] The McCarthy broadcast would "end the insulation"[133] of those associated with "See It Now." By attacking McCarthy they all — especially Murrow himself — would become fair game.

Destiny's hand elevated the drama level a notch higher — if that was possible — when McCarthy himself stormed into town on March 8th, the day before the broadcast, demanding air time to respond to Adlai Stevenson's critical comments of March 6, 1954. He coupled his demands with a chilling threat: The networks would grant him air time "or know what the law is." His rebuttal would be delivered at the Dutch Treat Club in Manhattan on March 9, 1954, as if to set the stage for Murrow's show, to be broadcast later that day at CBS's Fifth Avenue offices.

Outside events seemed to be adding an air of inexorability to the impending broadcast. In Washington, D.C., on March 8th, Republican Senator Ralph Flanders of Vermont, in a speech on the Senate floor, accused McCarthy of setting out to wreck the GOP and set up a one-man party: "He dons his war paint. He goes into his war dance...He goes forth to battle and proudly returns with the scalp of a pink Army dentist." (i.e. Peress).[134] The convergence of events leading up to the broadcast was uncanny.

On the morning of March 9, 1953 Paley called Murrow and told him to offer McCarthy reply time on the air. Murrow whole-heartedly agreed. Both men felt that not only was it the right thing to

---

[131] Murrow, Id.
[132] Id., p. 431.
[133] Id.
[134] The Congressional Record, March 9, 1954.

do, but it would also vividly lend the appearance of fair-mindedness to the broadcast.

On Sunday, March 7, 1953, Murrow, Friendly and the rest of the "See it Now" crew had arrived at the office early to begin the long countdown to the program scheduled for Tuesday night.

Murrow worked mainly alone in the cutting room, asking staffers to bring him one thing after another. The atmosphere was professional, intense and mostly serious, save an occasional burst of humor to cut the tension. When a member of the production crew asked Murrow what he planned to say in his narration, he answered, "No one man can terrorize a whole nation unless we are his accomplices."[135] A single voice from the crew rose above the others: "Mr. Murrow, it's been a privilege to have worked for you." What do you mean — to have worked?"[136] shouted Friendly — in a boisterous tone — eliciting laughter throughout the main work area.

On Sunday evening, Murrow and Friendly asked the assembled staff to vent their opinions. "Was there any reason," asked Friendly, "why they should not do the broadcast?"[137] Though some reservations were mildly voiced, no one spoke against doing the program or stated any reasons why the show should not be done. Years later Fred Friendly told an interviewer that even if there were opposition to the broadcast, it wouldn't have made any difference. "Nothing was going to keep that program off the air," said Friendly.

As for Murrow, rarely before had he been as hands-on in the creating and writing of a "See It Now" show. This was his broadcast — the report of his life — and he wouldn't stop until it bore his unique and indelible stamp.

On the evening of March 9th at 7:45 p.m., Murrow read the evening news as he did most week nights. The broadcast on Joseph McCarthy was to begin at 10:30 p.m. Murrow was going after McCarthy on live national television — the first American to do so — and he was geared up to give the performance of a lifetime.

---

[135] Murrow, Id., p. 431.
[136] Id.
[137] Id., p. 432.

At 10:30 after opening credits and announcements, Edward R. Murrow somberly faced the cameras and spoke to millions of viewers:

> "Good Evening."

> "Tonight See It Now devotes its entire half hour to a report on Senator Joseph R. McCarthy, told mainly in his own words and pictures. Because a report on Senator McCarthy is by definition controversial, we want to say exactly what we mean to say; and I request your permission to read from script whatever remarks Murrow and Friendly may make. If the Senator feels that we have done violence to his words or pictures, and desires, so to speak, to answer himself, an opportunity will be afforded him on this program."

Murrow then ran the first film clip of McCarthy speaking. His design for the broadcast was to trap the Senator in his own contradictions.

The film clip had McCarthy warning that if "this fight against communism" were to become a fight between America's two parties, one party would be destroyed — "and the Republic cannot survive very long under a one party system." The cameras then cut back to Murrow who stated, "But on February 4, 1954, the Senator spoke of one party's treason." He flipped a switch and McCarthy appeared again on video tape saying, "those who wear the label 'Democrat... carry "the stain of a historic betrayal."

So much for the virtue of a two-party system. Then there was McCarthy on film, brandishing alleged secret evidence of Democrats' duplicity, "never supposed to have seen the light of day." Pan back to Murrow, who without inflexion, identified it as a hearing transcript that anyone could buy for two dollars.

Millions sat with eyes glued to their TV sets, hanging on every word, as McCarthy again appeared, this time questioning a witness — "You know the Civil Liberties Union has been listed as a front for...the Communist Party." Then back to Murrow who intoned in his deep baritone voice, "The Attorney General's list (of subversive organizations) does not and never has listed the A.C.L.U. as subversive. Nor does the F.B.I. or any other federal government agency."

The electronic point-counterpoint of McCarthy's past statements, being dissected by Murrow live, continued with a re-run of a Milwaukee banquet held in December 1951, at which an apparently choked up and overwrought McCarthy lamented having been "smeared and bull whipped" by his enemies: "My cup and my heart are so full, I can't talk to you." Flash to Murrow live: "But in Philadelphia...his heart was so full, he could talk..." The footage then rolled to McCarthy's ebullient words at the Washington's Birthday celebration of earlier that year, when before a packed audience, he staged a reprise of his own bull-whipping cross-examination of General Zwicker at the then-recent McCarthy committee hearing. McCarthy's scornful reenactment evoked gales of laughter and applause, all at Zwicker's expense.

McCarthy's attack upon the press was next, as he appeared on screen characterizing his opponents in the press as "extreme left wing." Cut to Murrow reading from an editorial in the Chicago Tribune which was infuriated by McCarthy's attack upon the Army:

> "The unwarranted interference of a demagogue...the line must be drawn or McCarthy will become the government."

As if to confirm the Chicago Tribune's warning, McCarthy was shown boasting about how he had the Eisenhower Administration in his cross-hairs — pledging to call it as he saw it, "regardless of who happens to be President" — these words expressing a greater personal challenge to Ike than even had been made to Truman. McCarthy even quoted Shakespeare. Heaping derision upon Army Secretary Stevens, he is shown in a film clip saying, "Upon what meat does this our Caesar feed."

In one of the most biting and dramatic moments of the broadcast, Murrow turned McCarthy's words against him:

"And upon what meat does Senator McCarthy
feed...two stapes of his diet...the investigations,
protected by immunity, and the half-truth."

It all fell together smoothly in the experienced broadcaster's
hands, abetted by the skillful producers and technicians in the
control room. Style, substance and acumen were coalescing to
produce television's version of a work of art. So seamless was the
presentation that although it was a mixture of live commentary and
previously- filmed kinescope, it came across like a wholly-live
show.

As a lead-up to his carefully crafted summation — evoking the
mastery of a great trial lawyer — Murrow took pains to make clear
that he was not attacking the Senate's investigative power, but its
abuse...that "the line between investigating and persecuting is a very
fine one, and the Junior Senator from Wisconsin has stepped over it
repeatedly." Then making direct eye-contact with the camera, and
without looking at the teleprompter, Murrow summarized in the
manner of a government leader rather than a reporter:

"His primary achievement has been in
confusing the public mind, as between the
internal and external threats of Communism.
We must not confuse dissent with disloyalty.
We must remember always that accusation is
not proof and that conviction depends upon
evidence and due process of law.

We will not walk in fear, one of another. We
will not be driven by fear into an age of
unreason, if we dig deep in our history and in
our doctrine; and remember that we are not
descended from fearful men. Not from men
who feared to write, to speak to associate, and
to defend causes that were for the moment
unpopular. This is no time for men who oppose
Senator McCarthy's methods to keep silent —
or for those who approve. We can deny our

heritage and our history but we cannot escape responsibility for the result. There is no way for a citizen of a republic to abdicate his responsibility...The actions of the Junior Senator from Wisconsin have caused alarm and dismay amongst our allies abroad and given considerable comfort to our enemies. And, whose fault is that? Not really his. He didn't create this situation of fear, he merely exploited it; and rather successfully. Cassius was right. 'The fault, deer Brutus, is not in our stars, but in ourselves." "Good night and good luck."

The broadcast — one that would go down in history — was over. Murrow slumped in his seat.

The calls began pouring in. By 1:30 a.m., CBS New York had received more than 1000 telegrams, almost all of them approving. Western Union reported a huge backlog not yet processed.

The CBS switchboards were overloaded but more than 2000 calls had made it through, with hundreds more backed-up. Similar results were reported by CBS affiliates throughout the country. A groundswell of reaction was running as much as 10 to 1 against McCarthy and in favor of Murrow. It was the largest mass response ever generated by a single TV program. CBS New York was still flooded with phone calls 19 hours after the broadcast had ended.

The program was a flash point — a catalyst mobilizing both public opinion and the already-existent anti-McCarthy forces — principally but in no wise exclusively in the Executive Branch of the U.S. government.

The White House was also the recipient of a heavy flow of telegrams, mostly pro-Murrow and anti-McCarthy. The President and his lieutenants welcomed this unsolicited support as they geared up for the tough days ahead in their battle with McCarthy, at the Army — McCarthy hearings.

The more than 100,000.00 communications to CBS included thousands which contained the writer's names and addresses. Anonymity — a byproduct of America's fear — was being discarded everywhere. Murrow had sent them a message loud and clear — if someone of his prominence could say it on nation-wide television, it must now be safe for others to speak out-for attribution.

Typical of those in the press who shed their timidity in the wake of Murrow's ground-breaking broadcast was John Crosby of the New York Herald Tribune who wrote, "He [Murrow] put his finger squarely on the root of the true evil of McCarthyism, which is its corrosive effect on the souls of hitherto honest men..." And even pro-McCarthy newspapers gave the show unexpected attention:

The New York Daily News's banner headline of March 10, 1954 was,

> "McCARTHY GETS TV TIME OFFER. MURROW BLASTS
> SENATOR, MAKES BID."

The afternoon Journal-American, a Hearst publication, ran a simpler and more succinct but massive headline:

> "TELECAST RIP AT McCARTHY STIRS STORM."

Murrow was mobbed by adulatory crowds on his way back from lunch the next day in midtown Manhattan. Variety Magazine called Murrow "practically a national hero." Fifteen hundred attendees at an annual national press dinner that month stood and gave Murrow a spontaneous standing ovation as he entered the room.

Alistair Cook called the response "a stunning endorsement of Murrow's Courage."[138] He wrote:

> "Hence the surprising rally of candor in public men who have stayed silent for 5 years. Hence President Eisenhower's relieved approval of Senator Flanders. Hence a morning chorus of... newspaper columnists praising Murrow for 'laying it on the line.' Hence the confident laughter in yesterday's subcommittee hearing...Mr. Murrow may yet make bravery fashionable."[139]

---

[138] The Guardian Weekly.
[139]

Columnist Joseph Alsop was equally effusive in his praise, telegramming Murrow that his "See It Now" performance was "ONE OF THE GREAT ACTS OF POLITICAL COURAGE OF OUR TIMES."

The praise was not, however, unanimous. Gilbert Seldes of the Saturday Review, accused Murrow of "stacking the deck and setting a dangerous example..."[140]

Variety called the program an expedient of great interest, and some belated courage, but basically...a footnote to history rather than a definitive answer to McCarthyism...[141] Other editorial writers and columnists wrote similar critiques. Most of the negative reviews, however, fell into the category of either Murrow's having gone too far, or not far enough. Very few of them took serious issue with the accuracy of the show's content.

Murrow's most enthusiastic support came from Europe. As one foreign correspondent put it, "The European newspapers went crazy, they were delighted; it was like America coming into its own again."[142]

The State Department seemed to emit a collective sigh of relief. It had for months embraced a bunker mentality, as first the V.O.A. and the U.S.I.A. had come under attack from McCarthy; and more recently, its military attachés and the Army itself.

Praise for Murrow came from all parts of the country — even McCarthy's midwest, where many still remembered fondly Murrow's "This is London" reports during the worst of the Blitz. Typical of the strongly positive reaction was a cartoon in the Cleveland Plain Dealer which "depicted a jowly McCarthy staggering in defeat, with an object labeled 'Murrow's Mike' wrapped lethally around his neck."[143]

Murrow was to the Eisenhower — McCarthy war what Lafayette was to the American Revolution. In either case the war might have been won without his help, but one shudders to think what could have happened had the help not come when it did. Murrow had what

---

[140] Murrow, Id., p. 441.
[141] Murrow, Id.
[142] Id.
[143] Murrow, Id., p. 443.

we refer to today as "gravitas". Putting his full weight publicly on the line against McCarthy did the Senator incalculable damage.

On Thursday evening, March 11, 1954, McCarthy struck back. On the Fulton Lewis, Jr. program — billed as a response to the criticism by Adlai Stevenson — McCarthy's strongest words were aimed at Murrow:

> "If I may say, Fulton," intoned McCarthy, "that I have a little difficulty answering the specific attacks...because I have listened to the extreme left-wing bleeding-heart elements on radio and television........I have in my hand a copy of the Pittsburgh Sun-Telegram [sic]; it's dated February 18, 1935....'The Moscow University taught' if I may quote from [the story], "the violent overthrow of the entire traditional social order'..."

McCarthy's uncanny ability to make a big publicity splash did not disappoint. He deftly got the story on the wires in time for the Friday morning editions of the Nation's newspapers. McCarthy's sense of timing proved superior to Murrow's whose Friday evening point-by-point reply was mostly swamped by the cascade of pre-weekend news. This time it was McCarthy who got the splashy headlines; Chicago Tribune: "McCARTHY...STRIKES BACK AT EDWARD MURROW"; The Dallas Morning News: "McCARTHY CLAIMS MURROW TAINTED."

The power of McCarthy's headlines and favorable commentary in the pro-McCarthy newspapers was, however, muted and diluted by the Eisenhower Administration. On Friday morning, its bomb-shell dominated the morning press. Causing the stir was the report of the U.S. Army, containing detailed allegations of multiple strong-armed tactics employed by McCarthy.

Events were moving at a breath-taking pace. McCarthy committee Democrats had staged a mini-rebellion on Thursday, protesting what they claimed was McCarthy's badgering of a witness." On the same day, Eisenhower met with the press and commended Senator Flanders for his blistering verbal assault upon

McCarthy. Just in case anyone missed the point, Ike ordered transcripts of his comments released to the media. In his oblique manner, he had taken a clear slap at McCarthy.

Murrow had started the onslaught on Tuesday. By Friday the McCarthy story was completely dominating the news. On Sunday, March 14, the New York Times Week in Review spread a photo gallery across a page depicting the principal players: Murrow top-row center, flanked by McCarthy and Flanders: Then Roy Cohn, Secretary Stevens and an unsmiling President Eisenhower.

McCarthy had taken a hit to his popularity, although by no means a fatal one. A new Gallup Poll registered a significant dip in McCarthy's approval rating from its all-time high in January of 1954.

At the Washington Correspondents' Dinner in Washington, D.C., the well-connected and keenly observant Joseph Alsop witnessed a momentary incident which spoke volumes. He noticed Ike approach Murrow from behind and place one hand on his back. Alsop then saw Eisenhower come around Murrow to face him, wearing the famous Eisenhower grin- from ear to ear. "Just feeling to see if there were any knives sticking in it," said the President — his humorous remark followed by boisterous laughter by both Ike and Murrow. "From here on in," Murrow replied, "it's up to you Mr. President."

In the aftermath of the landmark broadcast, Murrow and his wife, Janet, were swamped with threats and hate-mail. They genuinely feared for the safety of their school-age son, Casey.

The New York Daily Mirror's resident poet, Nick Kenny, wrote a poem entitled "The Commy-tator":

> *"He glasses quickly over news*
> *That sounds red, white and blue*
> *And saves his drooling, pear-shaped tones*
> *For Communistic goo.*
>
> *Yet how he still goes on,*
> *Polluting freedom's air,*
> *This worm whose body's over here*
> *But whose heart is over there."*

In his televised response of April 5, 1954 to Murrow, on CBS, McCarthy made good use of the twenty two minutes allotted to him. The famous — some preferred "infamous" — reporter and columnist, Drew Pearson, called McCarthy's rebuttal "a savage and effective job." McCarthy had described Murrow as "a symbol, the leader and the cleverest of the jackal pack which is always found at the throat of anyone who dares to expose individual communists and traitors." He went on to colorfully accuse Murrow of having been a leader in alleged Communist front organizations controlled by the Soviet Union. In an exercise of vintage McCarthyism he sought to condemn Murrow by listing the names of alleged communists who had praised him, such as Owen Lattimore and Victor Lasky.

Then taking a gratuitous swipe at the Administration, McCarthy charged that Communists in government had fatally held up research on the H bomb, and as a consequence, "our nation may well die."

Eisenhower felt constrained to deny the charge. Typical of the next day's headlines was, "IKE OK's H-BOMB SPEED-UP."

McCarthy kept up a relentless barrage against Murrow — his biggest attack line being that Murrow gives "aid and comfort to the enemy." He cited no specific instances of how he had done such a thing other than his "See it Now" attack upon McCarthy. But McCarthy picked up some impressive editorial support from the Chicago Tribune, The New York Daily Mirror and the New York Journal American.

The March 9, 1954 Murrow broadcast had galvanized both the pro and anti-McCarthy forces like nothing before it. Public attention to the raging controversies spawned by McCarthyism grew exponentially between March 9 and April 6, the date of McCarthy's response on CBS. The advance publicity for the April 6th program produced a quantum leap in viewership. McCarthy was staging a fierce counter attack and producing results. But Murrow was hanging tough also. On April 7 the New York Times reported that E.R. Murrow was leading all other candidates for the New York Newspaper Guild's prestigious Page One Awards.

The irony of the situation was that it was a private citizen, not a public official, who had decided to go after McCarthy full bore. Murrow seemed to have become the lightning rod for the McCarthy forces, by the law of unintended consequences. As understandable as the President's strategy was, of not mentioning McCarthy by name, but letting him self-destruct, it's hard to imagine that Ike would have intended to have the high ground of one of the major public issues of the day preempted by a newsman. But that's what happened. No one could have known, however, on April 6, 1954, that the McCarthy — Murrow battles would eventually be eclipsed by a far bigger and more decisive political war, which came to be known as the Army-McCarthy hearings.

For the time being in March and early April, it was Murrow, Friendly and their "See It Now" broadcasts which were the flashpoints of the McCarthy opposition. Ike did, however, get the opportunity to weigh in. At a White House news conference, Eisenhower was pointedly asked for a comment on the loyalty and patriotism of Edward R. Murrow. With a combination of circumspection and guile, the President said he wouldn't comment on things of which he "knew nothing," but he had known this man for many years and considered him to be "a friend." The afternoon edition of the New York Post parlayed the response into a headline in huge black letters, "IKE BACKS MURROW, CALLS JOE'S TARGET HIS FRIEND." Murrow was relieved and grateful. But on March 12, 1954 — spurred on by extensive sub rosa leaks of McCarthy files to the FBI — the Bureau began an investigation of Edward R. Murrow. He became a watched man. His FBI dossier in 1951 consisted of about three quarters of one page and chiefly reflected J. Edgar Hoover's view of Murrow as a first rate newsman. By the end of 1954, Murrow's dossier consisted of scores of pages of investigative reports and exhibits. On the surface nothing changed. For the rest of the 1950's and into the early 60's, Murrow continued to be one of the top TV personalities in America, eventually named by President Kennedy as head of the United States Information Agency. Beneath the surface, however, Murrow was viewed with distrust by the FBI — mostly because of what J. Edgar Hoover viewed as an unsavory association with leftist organizations and long-time affiliations with reportedly left-leaning individuals, such as Quentin Reynolds, Theodore White and Owen Lattimore.

Ed Murrow's reputation as the venerable dean of the U.S. press corps was never publicly sullied. In the deep recesses of the FBI, however, and perhaps of other investigatory bodies, he was darkly viewed — his credentials as a patriot suspect.

The legacy of the Murrow-McCarthy wars almost sixty years later has greater clarity. The allegations, accusations, rejoinders and counterattacks from both camps added to the intellectual ferment of mid-to-late 20th Century America and became distilled down to a new formulaic view of the meaning of a democracy. A Protestant minister from Harrison, New York was captured on See-It-Now in 1954 quoting Justice Learned Hand to characterize McCarthyism. In his sermon, he said:

> "Where nonconformity with the accepted creed is a mark of disaffection, where denunciation takes the place of evidence, where orthodoxy chokes freedom of dissent...those who begin coercive elimination of dissent, soon find themselves exterminating dissenters."

Prior to Murrow — McCarthy, the term "civil liberties" had come to be equated with subversion, in a significant region of the public mind. The Murrow-McCarthy charges and counter-charges riveted the public's attention on fundamental concepts embodied in the Declaration of Independence and U.S. Constitution. Most were revisiting these concepts. Some seemed to focus on them for the first time. With McCarthy-Murrow there was an awakening as to a national moral issue, a new understanding of the intrinsic value of free speech, free association and due process of law.

Murrow distilled the issue further as to the question of the hour, in his broadcast of Edward R. Murrow with the News on May 28, 1954:

> "The issue...has finally been joined. It is constitutional and therefore fundamental..."

By May 28, 1954 the forum had already shifted to the Senate Caucus Room where the Senate Permanent Sub-Committee on

Investigations, unlike Murrow-McCarthy, was not conducting a debate. Rather they were engaged in a no-holds-barred power-struggle which not all would survive.

The Murrow phase of the McCarthy saga was winding down. On May 29, 1954, White House Press Secretary James Hagerty sent Murrow a note on White House letterhead expressing the White House's gratitude for his May 28 broadcast: "Many thanks, you were wonderful."

The American public was still divided on McCarthyism, but as to Murrow, the comment of reporter-columnist, Jack Gould, on April 7, 1954 seemed to reflect the prevailing sentiment in America: "Mr. Murrow only reported as best he could on the use of innuendo, insinuation, the half-truth and the frantic smear."[144]

---

[144] <u>Murrow</u>, Id., p. 449.

CHAPTER EIGHT

Ike and McCarthy

The forerunner of the Army — McCarthy hearings was the Fall, 1953 inquiry by the Senate Subcommittee on Investigations into suspected Communist infiltration of the U.S. Army Signal Corps at Fort Monmouth, New Jersey. The investigation produced no tangible results but an incident which occurred during the same time-frame triggered an explosive confrontation between McCarthy and the Army, attracting nation-wide media attention.

Irving Peress, a New York dentist, was drafted by the Army in 1952 at the rank of Captain. He was assigned to Camp Kilmer, New Jersey, as one of the facility's dental officers. In November, 1953, he was promoted to the rank of major by his commanding officer, then-Colonel Ralph W. Zwicker.

Shortly after his promotion, the Army bureaucracy focused for the first time on the fact that Peress, a member of the leftward-leaning American Labor Party, had declined to answer questions about his political affiliations on the Military's loyalty-review form. U.S. Army Command ordered that Peress be discharged from the Army within thirty days.

While Peress's discharge was pending, McCarthy issued a subpoena to him to appear and give testimony before the Senate Subcommittee on Investigations, on January 30, 1954.

Appearing with counsel at the January 30th session, Peress refused to answer McCarthy's questions on the grounds of his right against self-incrimination under the Fifth Amendment to the U.S. Constitution.

McCarthy sent a letter to Robert T. Stevens, Secretary of the Army, demanding that Peress be court-martialed. Peress countered that same day by asking that his pending discharge be made effective immediately. The next day Peress's commanding officer, Ralph W. Zwicker, who had been promoted to the rank of Brigadier General, awarded Peress an honorable discharge from the Army.

McCarthy was furious and expressed his anger publicly, loudly and often. Following McCarthy's cue, thousands of his supporters adopted the rallying cry, "Who promoted Peress?" The Peress affair had become a cause célebré — setting off a tempest of protest. McCarthy himself did not adopt the rallying cry but did nothing to discourage his followers from using it.

In fact, the actual answer to the question, "Who promoted Peress?" was that Peress had been promoted automatically under the provisions of the Doctor Draft Law, for which McCarthy had voted.

The controversy grew. McCarthy subpoenaed General Zwicker to appear before his subcommittee on February 18, 1954. The events of the McCarthy-Zwicker confrontation are treated earlier in Chapter Seven of this book.

Antagonism between McCarthy and the Army grew incrementally with each passing day.

McCarthy — still fuming — demanded that Secretary Stevens block an overseas posting for Private G. David Schine, a top McCarthy aide, who had been drafted into the Army, in November, 1953. When Stevens refused to intervene, McCarthy charged that the United States Army was "soft" on Communism.[145] And to demonstrate that he was not all bark and no bite, McCarthy's committee launched an all-out investigation of Communist

---

[145] History.com.this-day-in-history/McCarthy-Army Hearings begin.

infiltration of the Army. Eisenhower was of course, indignant, but again hid his indignation from the public, while venting to his staff and advisers.

Eisenhower's public reticence did not in any way reflect his long-festering resentments toward McCarthy. It was one thing for McCarthy to fire off inane brick bats at the V.O.A., the Protestant Churches and the CIA, thought Eisenhower, but when he attacked the U.S. Army, an institution near and dear to Ike's heart, and then hauled senior Army officers before his committee to abuse and humiliate them, that was the last straw. From then on it was all-out war between Ike and McCarthy.

That the occasion, however, for the final battle between Senator McCarthy and the White House was a slow-simmering yet combustible rift with the U.S. Army, seems fortuitous when viewed through the lens of history.

Of all the issues over which Ike and McCarthy had clashed — General Marshall, Presidential appointments, Communists in the State Department, the CIA and many others — a climactic showdown with the Army might have been the most difficult to predict. McCarthy was a veteran of World War II and enjoyed much genuine support in the armed forces. But the Army — McCarthy conflict happened to be front and center and conveniently — though coincidentally visible — when the hostility between the President and the Senator reached critical mass. It could have been any one of multiple disagreements between the two men but Army — McCarthy provided the scene for the final reckoning; because when the volatile estrangement hit its apogee, that was the forum which just happened to be in place.

Schine's induction into the Armed Forces occurred contemporaneously with the onset of a "personal campaign" by Roy Cohn to pressure the military into giving Private Schine special privileges.[146] Schine and Cohn were close personal friends. Cohn was also a closet homosexual. The vehemence of Cohn's campaign in 1953-54 to gain favorable treatment for Schine, the young and

---

[146] The Museum of Broadcast Communications, www.museum.tv/archives,McCarthy/Army.

handsome bachelor with whom Cohn shared an apartment, led to speculation concerning a possible homosexual relationship between them. No conclusive proof was ever presented of such a relationship. But the rumors seeped into the fabric of the Army-McCarthy hearings and affected the atmosphere within which they took place.

The preliminary skirmishes between McCarthy and the Army seemed to have gone McCarthy's way. The low point for the Army was the infamous "Chicken Luncheon." Afterward, McCarthy boasted to a reporter that Secretary Stevens "could not have given in more abjectly if he got down on his knees."[147] Pentagon officers were aghast at Stevens's acts of appeasement and widely ridiculed him. The Times of London wrote: "Senator McCarthy achieved today what General Burgoyne and General Cornwallis never achieved — the surrender of the American Army."[148]

While McCarthy smugly basked in what ultimately proved to be a pyrrhic victory, the President brooded alone, in the White House. But as he brooded, he calculated and planned. Of the many miscalculations made by McCarthy, the biggest one was poking the sleeping lion in the oval office.

On March 11, 1954, Ike struck back with a fury. With at least his full encouragement and support, the Army leveled charges against McCarthy that he and his chief counsel, Roy Cohn, improperly pressured the Army to grant special privileges to Private G. David Schine.

The charges were serious. A United States Senator was being accused of abusing his power and engaging in an unseemly conflict of interest. If the allegations were true, McCarthy-Cohn had sought to corrupt one of America's venerable institutions, by coercing the Army into coddling a top McCarthy aide and favoring him with special treatment. By the power of McCarthy's largesse, Schine would have become the most pampered Private in the United States Army — and all less than a year after the cease fire in the Korean War — a brutal conflict in which almost forty thousand American

---

[147] Wikipedia.org/JosephMcCarthy.
[148] Id.

servicemen died, and hundreds of thousands more were wounded or captured.

The charges were made on March 11, 1954 in an explosive written chronology documenting in detail a wide-spread campaign to unduly pressure everyone from the Secretary of the Army down to Schine's company commander. They were similar in form to a criminal indictment with no concessions made to the niceties of politics. Illustrative of the tenor of the charges in the chronology was one in which Cohn was said to have signed McCarthy's name without his knowledge on a request form for Schine to have access to the Senators' baths.

Even McCarthy acknowledged that Cohn was unreasonable in matters involving Schine, but he chose to make no concessions to the Army's charges. "The Army," bellowed McCarthy "was holding Schine 'hostage'" to deter his committee from exposing communists within the military ranks. And the accusations were made in "bad faith" by the Army, said McCarthy. They were, according to his estimation, nothing more than "retaliation" for his aggressive questioning of General Zwicker a few months earlier.

One cannot say with absolute certainty that the Army's motive was not retaliation. But, historical integrity requires attention to a few additional facts before rendering judgment. First, McCarthy's investigation of alleged communist infiltration of the Army did not end with the Zwicker-Peress affair of late 1953. When the Army released its accusatory document on March 11, 1954, the McCarthy investigation was fully active and showed no signs of winding down any time soon. McCarthy never showed the slightest sign of softening his accusation that the Army was "soft on Communism." If anything, his invective against the Army — and indirectly against the Eisenhower Administration — had grown more strident.

Both McCarthy and Cohn often expressed their desire for their friend and aide, G. David Schine, to be excused from the ho-hum training and military details to which other draftees and new recruits were subjected. They considered Schine to be too important a man for such trivial duties. Their desire was to have Schine assigned after Basic Training to an Army investigative unit. Once in place there, Schine would be used to investigate communist subversion, from the inside. Hence McCarthy's indignation when Secretary Stevens refused to cooperate. McCarthy, a shrewd political animal, had to know that Stevens was too weak to act on his own, and was probably carrying out the orders of the White House.

G. David Schine was, in many ways, the alter ego of Joe McCarthy and Roy Cohn. When they demanded that he be treated as a special case, they were also making a statement about how they should be treated. Whether it was because of hubris, arrogance, a sense of the nobility of their mission, self-importance, lust for power or any combination thereof, their actions bespoke an attitude which was that they were not bound by the conventions and rules governing ordinary men. How their attitude was perceived in the Oval Office — occupied by one of the greatest military leaders of the 20th Century — can only be partially gleaned from Ike's public utterances and writings. Eisenhower adhered strictly to his own injunction against "getting down in the gutter" with McCarthy. Fortunately for the sake of history, a body of empirical evidence exists which documents many of his private and candid thoughts and feelings on the subject.

On March 10, 1954, the day before the Army issued its list of grievances against McCarthy, Ike held a press conference. For public consumption, he again voiced his opposition to McCarthy's efforts to censor books at Army libraries. As to Adlai Stevenson's charge that the GOP was "a house divided-half Eisenhower and half McCarthy" — all he would say was "nonsense". Privately, however, Ike designated Vice President Richard M. Nixon to respond to Stevenson's charges. To a few top advisors, Eisenhower was more expansive on what had become one of his favorite subjects: the positions and actions of the junior senator from Wisconsin.

The diary entries of White House Press Secretary James Hagerty for March 10, 1954 are a case in point: "Pres in fighting mood," wrote Hagerty, "has had it as far as Joe is concerned." "If he (McCarthy) wants to get recognized anymore," said Ike to his aide, Jerry Persons, the "only way he can do it is to stand up and publicly say, I was wrong in browbeating witnesses, wrong in saying the Army is coddling Communists, and wrong in my attack on Stevens. I apologize." And Ike said decisively, "that's (sic,"the") only way I (sic "will") welcome him back in the fold." The Eisenhower-McCarthy relationship had become surreal. Only fourteen months into a presidency which presumptively would last eight years, Joe McCarthy had managed to have himself declared persona non grata by the leader of the free world, the highly renowned head of McCarthy's own political party. This was not exactly a positive precursor for the rest of McCarthy's political career. Little did the Senator know then that when the live television coverage of the Army-McCarthy hearings began on ABC, with the slamming of acting-committee chairman Karl Mundt's gavel on April 22nd, it was not so much McCarthy's future which was at stake as his present. Still hopeful of eventually being the GOP's candidate for president, McCarthy seemed clueless about the fact that that train had already left the station. Had he realized how tenuous his true position was, he might have used the hearings as a forum for a show of statesmanship; to repair his image and to mend some broken fences. He did neither of those things.

Contemporaneously, Eisenhower's ire was frequently raised not only by McCarthy but also by members of his own administration. He would often complain to intimates about how senior officials were mishandling and coddling McCarthy.

When Secretary of Defense Charles E. Wilson, a former captain of industry, sent his own car to pick up McCarthy for a luncheon at the Pentagon; and neglected to even tell the White House about the luncheon, Eisenhower was irate. When informed of the event by Hagerty, the President leaned back in his chair, muttered a few 'goddams' and then said, 'You know, Jim, I believe Cabot Lodge is dead right when he says we need acute politicians in those positions. They are the only ones who know enough to stay out of traps — the only ones who can play the same kind of game as those guys on the Hill.'"[149]

That neither Ike nor any of his lieutenants were informed of the meeting was a cause for great concern by the President. Afterwards he called Hagerty several times for news as to what occurred at the

---

[149] Minutes of Meeting between James Hagerty and the President, Id., 3/10/54.

luncheon. The Administration had already been burned once by the "Chicken Luncheon" with Secretary Stevens and the last thing the President wanted was an encore. "If they are cooking up another statement," said Eisenhower, "then, by God someone is going to hear from me — but good." These were fighting words, reminiscent of meetings with Generals Brook, Bradley, Montgomery and Patton during World War II.

News of the Wilson-McCarthy interview finally broke over the wire services and it was reported that Joe McCarthy had supposedly "pulled in his horns." Ike was not impressed: "Just a lot of words. No use to have that luncheon at all."[150]

On March 24, 1954, as the McCarthy Committee-now with Senator Karl Mundt as acting chairman-was hard at work on the preliminaries to the television coverage, an internal debate raged in the White House. A bitter argument broke out between Jim Hagerty and Jerry Persons. Persons was aghast at Hagerty's opinion that the President should take a stand on whether McCarthy should stay on the committee during the Army hearings, and if so, whether he should have the right to cross-examine witnesses. "It's a matter for the Senate," argued Persons, and the President "should not get into it."[151] Persons was so angry he didn't even come to the staff meeting at which a recommendation to the President was being debated.

The argument continued at the staff meeting — with the President's staff divided into two camps — the proponents for Person's position and those for Hagerty's position, the crux of which was that the President was not only a political leader but a moral leader too. For that reason he "would get murdered," argued Hagerty,[152] if he didn't express himself on the question.

At the subsequent meeting with the President himself, Ike stopped the advocates for his non-involvement "dead in their tracks."[153] "Look, I know exactly what I'm going to say," said Ike. "I'm going to say he (McCarthy) can't sit as a judge and that the leadership can't duck that responsibility. I've made up my mind you

---

[150] Id.
[151] Id., March 24, 1954.
[152] Id.
[153] Id.

can't do business with Joe and to hell with any attempts to compromise."[154]

Later, in the presidential limousine on the way to a press conference, the President looked at Hagerty with a smile on his face. The smile morphed into a laugh as the President spoke: "The two Jerrys (i.e. presidential aides) didn't look very happy this morning." Not wishing to comment on his colleagues, Hagerty decided to duck the question. But Ike was not finished with the point he was making and would not change the subject: "I know, Jim. Listen, I'm not going to compromise my ideals and personal beliefs for a few stinking votes. To hell with it." Out of the hurly burly of the campaign, followed by almost fifteen months in the White House, one of those rare, magical moments had emerged. Hagerty felt a pleasant warmth spread throughout his body. It provided the well-spring for his emotion-filled response: "Mr. President, I'm proud of you."[155]

---

[154] Id.
[155] Id.

CHAPTER NINE

The Army — McCarthy's Hearings

The mandate given by the U.S. Senate to the Permanent Subcommittee on Investigations was to adjudicate the conflicting charges between McCarthy and the Army. The committee was normally chaired by McCarthy himself but the senate decided that it would be highly inappropriate under the circumstances, since his conduct was included within the matters under investigation. The job of chairman thus went to a reluctant Senator Karl Mundt of South Dakota.

The televised Army-McCarthy hearings convened on April 22, 1954. Army Secretary Robert T. Stevens and Senator Joseph R. McCarthy were the principal targets of the proceedings — Stevens, the McCarthy camp's target; and McCarthy, the Army's target.

The hearings were broadcast live "gavel to gavel" on the ABC and DuMont networks. An air of excitement hung over the Senate hearing room as Senator Mundt lowered his gavel for the first time on April 22nd. The sharp report of wood upon wood was to become as common as McCarthy's plaintive, "Mr. Chairman, Point of Order!", during the next thirty-six days. The names of men who were largely unknown to the American public before the hearings — such as Army Counsel, John G. Adams; Army Special Counsel,

Joseph N. Welch; Committee Chief Counsel, Roy Cohn, and McCarthy consultant, G. David Schine — became household words during the tumultuous hearings and their aftermath. An estimated 80 million people saw at least part of the hearings, which were televised coast to coast.

It was an uncommon role for Joe McCarthy to be a contestant and an accused at an adjudicatory hearing of what had been — up until April 22, 1954 — his own tightly-controlled fiefdom. McCarthy's discomfiture over being target rather than interrogator seemed to drive his repeated use of the mantra, "Point of Order". Live television served to accentuate McCarthy's odd, nervous giggle and his tendency to sweat profusely when confronted with hostile questioning. It was not an attractive picture.

The televised hearings continued for a grinding thirty-six days in the Senate Caucus room. "During one hundred and eighty eight hours of broadcast, the American public witnessed a spectacle of high drama, embarrassing disclosures, inflamed resentments and vitriolic exchanges between the protagonists of the opposing sides.

The networks' feed to NBC, ABC and DuMont came courtesy of ABC's Washington, D.C. affiliate, WMAL-TV. The nation-wide exposure of Joe McCarthy on television at a time before media-imaging had evolved into an art-form, was unforgiving. He generally came across on T.V. as boorish and rude; while Ray Cohn's interminable and unctuous posturing made him unappealing as well to the vast T.V. audience. On style points they were clearly at a disadvantage to the bow-tie adorned, patrician-mannered and coolly avuncular Joseph M. Welch, a partner of the prominent Boston law firm of Hale and Dorr, whom the Army had engaged as special counsel.

Other hitherto obscure Washington staffers were transformed as well from anonymity to celebrity almost overnight. They included the often feckless Army Secretary Robert T. Stevens, the Chain-smoking Committee Counsel, Ray H. Jenkins, and the tightly-wound and subtly menacing counsel for the Committee Democrats, Robert F. Kennedy.

The drama played out before a partisan gallery in the packed, smoke-filled hearing room and a television audience of some twenty-million Americans. It was not all riveting theater. Some witnesses droned on through ponderous testimony, weaving tedious and abstruse fact patterns of such complexity as to be incomprehensible to most viewers. Then, unexpectedly, boring testimony would yield to a crossfire of recriminations by both sides over allegations of eavesdropped telephone conversations, doctored photographs and fabricated writings. Two million words of testimony over 36 days provided ample opportunities for such interludes of high drama. The players did not disappoint.

The hearings revealed the drama and conflict publicly. Two revered institutions, the U.S. Army and the U.S. Senate, were gripped in an unprecedented public blood-letting. But so controversial and polarizing a figure was Joe McCarthy that a sense of inevitability permeated the proceedings.

A third bulwark of American government, The White House, was also far from immune from the controversy and drama. Unknown to the Press and Public, heated and passionate discussions led by the President of the United States about the Army-McCarthy dispute had begun in earnest as early as February 25, 1954.

At a morning meeting on February 25, key White House staffers gave their exclusive attention to Stevens-McCarthy, described by James Hagerty as having "really kicked up a mess."[156] The steering group on the McCarthy controversy interrupted the meeting to get some badly-needed legal and political insight from William Rogers, and Vice President Richard Nixon. Afterwards, the staff meeting resumed in the East Wing of the White House where the group was joined by Republican Senator, Everett Dirkson. Of particular concern was the fact that at the previous day's hearing, Secretary Stevens had been hammered by several senators during his testimony. Hagerty entertained the prospect that Stevens had no idea what he was doing.

Led by White House Chief of Staff Sherman Adams, the steering group managed to wrest a commitment from Dirkson that he would "get Republican members of the Committee together and see if they

---

[156] White House Minutes of James Hagerty, Press Secretary 2/25/54, the Eisenhower Presidential Library and Museum.

could issue (an) additional statement, "(1.) that the committee had complete confidence in Stevens's 'integrity and ability; (2.) that he was pursuing a proper course of action in dealing with problems arising from the Peress case; (3.) action to be taken by Stevens after completion of the Inspector General's report made it evident (that it) may not be necessary to call any officers involved and (4.) if called, they would be treated with 'proper respect.'"[157]

As evidence of how Roy Cohn had become bête noire to the President's inner circle, they prevailed upon Senator Dirkson to work on both the Democrats and Republicans on the McCarthy Committee to persuade them to fire Cohn as chief counsel. His efforts in that regard were totally ineffectual. Equally futile were Dirkson's efforts at the behest of the White House inner circle to strip McCarthy of some of his powers by enacting a resolution stating that no subpoena could be issued by the committee except by majority vote. Hagerty's terse entry in his minutes summarized Dirkson's efforts to reverse McCarthy's status as a "one-man committee."[158]

"Dirkson couldn't deliver." Those three words carried a powerful meaning. A leader of the United States Senate, with a Republican sitting in the White House, was still powerless to strip away any of the almost dictatorial authority of the Junior Senator from Wisconsin, who Dirkson appointed as Chairman of a standing Senate subcommittee, in the first place.

Eisenhower was both infuriated and frustrated by the situation. His total alienation from McCarthy had grown incrementally, but gradually, over the past two years, beginning with the attack on George Marshall. In the late winter and early Spring of 1954, Ike's anger had reached its pinnacle.

Hagerty reported Ike's state of mind in simple language: "Pres. Very mad and getting fed up — it's his Army and he doesn't like McCarthy's tactics at all." In the late afternoon of February 25, the inner group was joined by Secretary Stevens and Vice President Nixon for purposes of preparing a statement criticizing the

---

[157] Id.
[158] Id.

McCarthy committee's treatment of the Army. When completed, Hagerty cleared it with the President who found it to be insufficiently tough. Ike made the language stronger and Hagerty released it to the Press at about 6:00 p.m.

As a battle-hardened newsman and political pro, Hagerty sensed that Eisenhower's candid words to him would be of historical significance and ought to be recorded verbatim for posterity. He thus ended his minutes of February 25, 1954 by quoting his boss directly:

> "Quotes — Ike on subject:
>
> 'this guy McCarthy is going to get into trouble over this. I'm not going to take this one lying down — My friends tell me it won't be long in this Army stuff before McCarthy starts using my name instead of Stevens. He's ambitious. He wants to be President. He's the last guy in the world who'll ever get there if I have anything to say.'"[159]

Ike left few doubts in the minds of his advisers that he took McCarthy's hectoring of the Army personally. McCarthy's ad hominem attacks on General Zwicker and Secretary Stevens had left Eisenhower in what his aides recognized as a feisty and combative mood. To the outside world the White House appeared as a remote temple of dispassionate governance. To those, however, who worked there every day — such as James Hagerty, Sherman Adams and C. D. Jackson — its serene exterior camouflaged an inner sanctum filled with contentiousness, taut nerves and a president with a short fuse whenever anyone spoke the name of Joe McCarthy. When Army Counsel John G. Adams testified during the Army-McCarthy hearings that "Cohn had threatened to wreck the Army,"[160] things only got worse. When Secretary Stevens was forced to sit on the witness stand for thirteen straight days of mostly hostile questioning, White House staffers were reluctant to bring the

---

[159] Id.
[160] Obituary, Roy Cohn: Bob Drogin, _____ 8/3/86

matter up to the President lest they trigger an explosion of temper which might engulf them in its wake.

Ironically, there had never been a wide ideological chasm between the President and the Senator. The main orientation of Ike's life had been to employ an inventive and personality-driven style, to coalesce divergent parties towards the accomplishment of common goals. In doing so he had employed a methodology built on professional acumen and personal politics. But his politics had been utilitarian rather than ideological. He was far more of an architect-engineer of victory than an ideologue. In the late 40's and early 50's he directed his innate soldier's orientation against the international communist movement, which he saw as the new enemy to be defeated. McCarthy's anti-communism was also more pragmatic than ideological and came to the fore in the same general period of time, beginning with his famous February, 1950 speech decrying Communists in the State Department.

McCarthy professed to be a philosophical conservative but his politics were mainly driven by personal ambition. Eisenhower's politics defied labels but he was certainly no liberal.

The main political difference between the two men stemmed from radically divergent points of view on how government should function. Eisenhower viewed the U.S. government and its Constitution as a force for fair and even-handed administration of the affairs of state — for effective management under the protection of the Bill of Rights. McCarthy saw government as a means to an end — a source for the aggressive pursuit of power. Fairness and truth had little to do with it. Thus, McCarthy had no qualms about maligning General Zwicker, a widely recognized U.S. hero of World War II, when Zwicker refused to divulge the content of classified files, believing properly, that he was barred by law from such disclosure:

> McCarthy: "Any man who refuses to give information is not fit to wear the uniform of his

country and is in the same category of the traitor whom he is protecting."[161]

McCarthy was hardly as passionate however, about the need for transparency and the disclosure of information a few months later when he was a target of the Army-McCarthy hearings. In May of 1954, he began pushing for the ongoing Army-McCarthy hearings to go into executive session with the witnesses testifying behind closed doors. Secretary Stevens, who was in the 13th day of very grueling and public testimony, cried foul. On behalf of the Army, he adamantly refused to take the hearings private.

White House aide, Jerry Persons, made the mistake on May 2, 1954 during a staff session with the President and others, of remonstrating to all present that Stevens had made a wrongheaded decision by refusing to let the hearing go into closed session. Not for the first time, Persons had underestimated Ike's irascibility when it came to McCarthy. In Hagerty's words, Ike "disagreed violently with Persons." "I think Stevens did exactly right" said Eisenhower. "Here he has been on the stand for 13 days and if his (McCarthy's) plan had been successful the other witnesses, except McCarthy, would have been testifying behind closed doors. McCarthy would then be at liberty to come out of the hearings and tell reporters anything he wanted....He would have a forum while the Army would not. Anyway I'm glad the Army is fighting him right down the line."[162]

Army Counsel John G. Adams testified that White House Chief of Staff, Sherman Adams, asked him to prepare a thorough memorandum on the Army-McCarthy case. Hagerty had apparently not been aware of this request and saw it as the beginning of active White House involvement. Equally significant, thought Hagerty, was that it presaged the thorny issue of how the White House would respond to a Committee subpoena of White House personnel, to testify at the hearings. Hagerty had more daily contact with Eisenhower than any other human being. He knew that the issue

---

[161] NBC <u>Nightly News</u>, Tom Brokow, Pete Williams, 5/5/03 NBS Universal Media, LLC.
[162] <u>Hagerty Minutes</u>, Id., 5/12/54.

would be trouble because concerning said subpoenas, Ike was unalterably opposed. Hagerty doubted that the President would ever permit it. The stage was set for a donnybrook with the Senate which would embrace the larger issue of the power of Congress versus that of the Executive branch.

The conflict began the very next day when Democratic Senator John L. McClellan, a member of the Committee, threatened to subpoena White House staff members to testify as to their interaction with Army personnel. McClellan was an imposing figure who later would gain fame as Chairman of the Senate Select Committee on Improper Activities in Labor and Management, which also conducted televised hearings and showcased a rising star in Washington, Chief Investigator and Chief Counsel, Robert F. Kennedy.

In the face of McClellan's threat, Ike immediately dug in his heals. Hagerty wrote in his White House minutes for May 14, 1954 that, "The President said that he would not stand for this for one minute." Eisenhower explained that "he looked upon his staff members as confidential advisors and that the Congress had absolutely no right to ask them to testify in any way, shape or form about the advice that they were giving to him at any time on any subject. "If they want to make a test of this principle," declared Eisenhower, "I'll fight them tooth and nail and up and down the country. It is a matter of principle with me and I will never permit it." To punctuate how strong and unbending were his convictions on the Army-McCarthy hearings, Ike then reiterated his belief that Secretary Stevens was "dead right" in refusing to permit the hearings from going into closed session. He would direct all of his staff members "to keep out of this controversy," to refuse to comment on it and to refer all questions dealing with McCarthy to Press Secretary Hagerty's office.

The President did not leave it there. Things had reached the point where no matter how remote from Joe McCarthy himself, was the topic under discussion, Ike did not ignore any opportunity to vividly express his disdain for the Senator. Hagerty, perhaps knowing that his White House minutes would someday become a significant historical document and a research source for historians and biographers, chose the safe route of quoting the President directly whenever the statement concerned McCarthy:

> "FRIDAY, MAY 14, 1954 (Cont'd)
>
> ...Ike — There is a phrase that a man is known by the friends he keeps. The other side of the coin is that a man is known by the enemies he makes. I read the last speech of Senator McCarthy. He said in that that we should have nothing to do with any nation that trades with the Reds. If he's against that, I'm for it."

Perennial presidential candidate Harold Stassen, who happened to be present at the May 14 meeting, commented that, "a lot of the talk on foreign trade dealt only with the British but that McCarthy, with a large Scandinavian population in his state, wouldn't dare make an attack against the Scandinavian countries dealing with the Reds."

Hagerty's minutes ended with the aforementioned Stassen quote, with apparently no dissenting voices heard concerning Stassen's vivid depiction of Joe McCarthy's apparent hypocrisy.

EVOLUTION OF EISENHOWER'S PRECEDENT ON EXECUTIVE PRIVILEGE

Most Americans who pay attention to events occurring on the National scene, associate the doctrine of "executive privilege" with President Richard M. Nixon, who in 1973 asserted it to prevent official investigators from obtaining evidence from the White House during the Watergate scandal. Yet nineteen years earlier, President Eisenhower had not only asserted the privilege during the Army-McCarthy hearings but had established an important precedent.

Ike made clear to his senior staff on numerous occasions after the Army-McCarthy hearings commenced that he would refuse to turn over White House papers and would not permit his personnel to testify before the Committee as to any communications between or among staffers, or between staffers and himself. The rationale was that matters of national security might be breached if administration officials were forced to testify under oath and/or the White House were to release to the Committee confidential documents, memoranda or communications.

As an example of the broad scope of the circle of protection, Ike made clear that he considered any communication whatsoever with White House Chief of Staff, Sherman Adams, to be a confidential communication with himself.

Eisenhower officially promulgated and expanded his executive privilege doctrine, thereby establishing it as a presidential precedent by his letter to the Secretary of Defense dated May 17, 1954.*

The crux of the Eisenhower doctrine on executive privilege is contained in the third paragraph of the letter which states the following:

> Because it is essential to efficient and effective administration that employees of the Executive Branch be in a position to be completely candid in advising with each other on official matters, and because it is not in the public interest that any of their conversations or communications, or any documents or reproductions, concerning such advice be disclosed, you will instruct employees of your Department that in all of their appearances before the Subcommittee of the Senate Committee on Operations regarding the inquiry now before it, they are not to testify to any such conversations or communications or to produce any such documents or reproductions. This principle must be maintained regardless of who would be benefited by such disclosure.

---

* See letter of May 17, 1954 from President Eisenhower to Secretary of Defense Wilson appended hereto as Appendix I.

In the next paragraph Eisenhower enunciated the underlying constitutional principle for his precedent.

> "I direct this action so as to maintain the proper separation of powers between the Executive and Legislative Branches of the Government..."

The letter also clearly broadened the privilege to include other departments of the Executive Branch. Then upon having the letter delivered by hand to the Defense Department, he met with the Congressional leadership and presented the doctrine to them as a fait accompli. He told them that he had sent the letter to the Secretary of Defense and that it was being made public as they spoke, by Press Secretary Hagerty's office.

In one master stroke which carried all the earmarks of Eisenhower's shrewd and calculating intellect, he had preempted the Congress, established an important precedent for his legacy and cut the ground out from under McCarthy's feet — all without giving anyone the opportunity to raise any serious opposition.

Journalists and historians latched onto the highly publicized televised confrontation between Army Special Counsel Welch and Senator McCarthy on June 9, 1954 as the high water mark of McCarthy's eclipse as a power to be reckoned with. But without fanfare, Ike had already plunged a dagger into the heart of McCarthyism, doing just as much damage.

By shutting down the Executive Branch to McCarthy's investigators and public interrogators-quietly but quickly and decisively-Ike robbed McCarthy of the opportunity to continue his inquisition in the invaluable forum provided to him — the nationally televised hearings in which he played the lead role. From that point on — after Ike invoked his broad policy of executive privilege — the Army-McCarthy hearings degenerated into a pitiful display of increasingly groundless and paranoid accusations. Without anything of substance to work with, McCarthy diminished himself to the point of buffoonery.

What bolstered Eisenhower's argument to Congress was his unwavering consistency in dealing with McCarthy over the seventeen months of his presidency. It had allowed him to comfortably state to the Congressional leaders "that they all knew he had been trying to stay out of the 'damn business on the Hill'; that many people have been begging him to get into the struggle and to attack McCarthy personally; but that he had refused to do so."[163]

However, said Ike, "a situation had come up in the threatened subpoena of his confidential advisors that made it necessary for him to act."[164]

Eisenhower proceeded to explain that he had written a letter to the Secretary of Defense, Charles E. Wilson, ordering him to refuse to permit Department officials to discuss confidential matters with the Committee, and that he had attached to it the Attorney General's memorandum outlining the precedents taken by twelve of his predecessors." "....Pseudo-liberals all over the country have been urging me to raise hell. I have not done that, but....any man who testifies as to the advice he gave me won't be working for me that night — - I will not allow people around me to be subpoenaed and you might just as well know it now..."[165]

By his decisive and definitive action on May 17, 1954, Eisenhower had trumped not only McClellan and the Democrats; McCarthy and his supporters, but also the entire Congressional leadership. By Ike's credible claim was that he had taken the high road all through the McCarthy controversies, had not interfered with Congress's prerogative and had declined to get into the "mess" even when needled by the press. He had carved out for himself an unassailable position. Paraphrased, it was, in essence, *I have not stuck my nose into your business so stay out of mine.* "I will not have my men subpoenaed."[166] Without ever publicly mentioning McCarthy by name during his presidency, Ike had managed to strike a crippling blow to McCarthy's career. Whether it would be fatal was not yet known on May 17, 1954.

Although Senate Majority Leader, William F. Knowland, expressed some reservations about the Executive Branch's undermining Congress's traditional subpoena power, he ultimately

[163] Id., May 17, 1954.
[164] Id.
[165] Id.
[166] Id.

agreed that the protection of confidential communications within the Executive Branch constituted a reasonable exception to subpoena power, provided it was not used to shield criminal or ethical wrongdoing.

Ike had adroitly backed McCarthy into a corner. Without the ability to subpoena White House and other Administration officials to testify at the Army-McCarthy hearings, McCarthy was bereft of his most effective tool: his ability to generate publicity. Since McCarthy had never been able to substantiate any of his charges, his loss of the controversy/publicity element had made him like the blind man whose seeing-eye dog had run away. From then on, his actions carried the whiff of desperation.

CHALLENGING THE PRESIDENTIAL AUTHORITY TO EXECUTE THE LAWS

Defiance born of desperation is often-times futile and sometimes destructive of the defiant himself. So it was that a desperate Joe McCarthy defied the authority of the President of the United States on Friday, May 27, 1954. And he did it in a most public way. At the Committee hearing on May 27, McCarthy boldly appealed to federal employees to disregard presidential orders and applicable laws and to ignore the President's pronouncement of executive privilege. Instead, such employees were urged to report directly to McCarthy himself any instances of "graft, corruption, communism and treason" within the Eisenhower Administration.

The reaction at 1600 Pennsylvania Avenue was not unexpected. Inciting government employees to disobey presidential orders was pushing hard at the boundaries of constitutionality beyond which resided anarchy. Would the Joe McCarthy of 1949 have committed such a provocative act? It seems doubtful. During the time period of 1950 through the first five months of 1954, McCarthy had repeatedly and without visible consequences provoked the powerful and powerless alike. Like tyrants and dictators, his power was a function of the quantum of fear he was able to instill. But by the Spring of 1954, McCarthy's view of himself had become skewed. Surrounded by sycophants and intoxicated by the aroma of success, he no longer saw himself objectively. But unlike dictators who can act with impunity so long as they can inflict confiscation of property, imprisonment, torture and death, McCarthy's capacity to instill fear was dependent upon a type of mass neurosis in America, born of what seemed like the inexorable movement towards world domination by Soviet Communism. Such movement was bolstered by U.S. internal subversion, the threat of nuclear annihilation and clear foreign policy reverses in Eastern Europe, China and Korea.

McCarthy had skillfully played upon the fears of Americans by piling the element of guilt on top. And, if he could raise a doubt in the minds of one's neighbors, friends, co-workers and employers that John Q. Public was a less than true-blue American; but rather was a pernicious Commie, Red, Pinko or Fellow-Traveler; then that individual's soul was no longer his — it belonged to Joe McCarthy.

The problem, however, for McCarthy was that he failed to see that America was slowly recovering from its neurosis. The healing medicines of perceived "peace and prosperity" wrought by the Eisenhower Administration, combined with McCarthy's unattractive personality traits — which included a perception of ruthlessness — were slowly healing of panic in America, at the same time that Americans were growing to dislike McCarthy. As more and more people began to see McCarthy's actions and words as extreme, overwrought and irrational — often the product of a man who imbibed too much liquor — their fears of him gradually began to recede. In inverse proportion to McCarthy's decline in popularity was Eisenhower's growth in popularity.

McCarthy, however, still had many staunch followers during the early stages of the Army-McCarthy Hearings. And the White House had far from discounted him as a force to be reckoned with.

The White House, May 28, 1954, 10:45 a.m.

A sense of urgency to counter McCarthy's latest gross overreaching permeated the West Wing of the White House:

Hagerty: "Here's our statement, Mr. President, on McCarthy's 'disregard presidential orders' plea."

President Eisenhower: "Why don't we get permission from the Attorney General, who after all is the first law enforcement officer in the country, to issue the statement in his name from the White House with my approval. In that way we will show that not only myself but my Administration condemns McCarthy's statement."

11:03 a.m.:

President Eisenhower: "Jim, please come back to my office."

Hagerty: "I'm on my way."

President Eisenhower: "I want to discuss this further." (He was clearly angry.) "The complete arrogance of McCarthy," said the President. The President then began "walking up and down behind his desk and speaking in rapid fire order." It seemed as though he had grown bigger and the Oval office smaller.

President Eisenhower: "This amounts to nothing but a wholesale subversion of public service. McCarthy is making exactly the same plea of loyalty to him, that Hitler made to the German people. Both tried to set up personal loyalty within the Government while both were using the pretense of fighting Communism. McCarthy is trying deliberately to subvert the people we have in government, people who are sworn to obey the law, the Constitution and their superior officers. I think this is the most disloyal act we have ever had by anyone in the Government of the United States."

Sitting down at his desk, the President seemed to be making a conscious effort to calm down: "I suppose I will be asked about this at my press conference."

Hagerty: "I'm sure it will come up."

President Eisenhower: "Make sure it does because I'll tell you what I'm going to say. I am going to tell the newsmen that in my opinion this is the most arrogant invitation to subversion and disloyalty that I have ever heard of. I am going to say — I am going to also say that if such an invitation is accepted by any employees of the Government and we find out who that employee is, he will be fired on the spot if a civilian and court martialed on the spot if a military man. I won't stand for it for one minute."

Hagerty: "I agree a hundred percent."

President Eisenhower: Well, would it be possible to feed a speech to Senator Potter to be delivered on the floor of the Senate on this subject?"

Hagerty: "I don't know. Maybe the best way would be for me to build up public opinion first."

President Eisenhower: "Good idea. I think you on your own should call certain key people that you know in radio, television and the newspapers to get this point of view over. And don't let anyone else in the White House know what you're doing.

4:30 p.m.: The South Lawn of White House

Hagerty: "I accomplished my mission. You might want to listen particularly to Ed Murrow's program at 7:45 tonight."

President Eisenhower: (while hitting golf balls) "Well, I'm going to the Ethiopian dinner this evening but will try to listen. This is a fundamental fight and one which I am sure we can win, but one to which I am also sure we will have to give a lot of attention to see that our point of view is accurately reflected in radio, television and the papers and throughout the country."

The Murrow broadcast of May 28, 1954

Before the Murrow T.V. program aired, Hagerty spent a productive afternoon reaching out by phone to a number of friendly journalists, to whom he read the key parts of the White House statement sanctioned by President Eisenhower and Attorney General Brownell: "He cited the separate functions of the three branches of government, blasting by implication a certain unnamed 'individual' seeking to 'usurp' executive responsibility, 'to set himself above the laws of our land...to override orders of the President of the United States."[167]

In each call to the media, Hagerty framed the dispute as flowing from a "constitutional issue," concerning which the President was completely right and McCarthy was lamentably wrong.

Murrow was atypically philosophical and somewhat above the fray in his May 28th broadcast, the major portion of which was,

> "The issue...has finally been joined. It is constitutional and therefore fundamental...clearly defined by the President of the United States on one hand and the Junior Senator from Wisconsin on the other. It can be simply stated. Who is going to run the government of this country? There have been times in our history when the executive...has attempted to dominate the legislature...There have been times when the Congress has made inroads on the prerogative of the Executive. What is here involved is whether a single senator shall publicly recruit and legalize what might be called a private Gestapo within the ranks of those employed by the federal government."[168]

The next day, Murrow received a note from Hagerty written on White House stationery:

> "Many thanks, you were wonderful."[169]

The hearings were gradually but emphatically changing from "Joe versus the Army" to "Joe versus Ike".[170]

---

[167] Murrow, Id., p. 468.
[168] Edward R. Murrow With the News, CBS News, 5/28/54.
[169] Murrow, Id., p. 469.
[170] Id., 468.

Considering how far McCarthy had come in public life in a span of only four and a half years, his miscalculations during the period beginning late April and culminating in early June 1954, were astounding. First, there was his shrill demand to compel by subpoena the attendance of the president's Advisors before the Committee. Next came his futile demand for Army files and finally, in a burst of hubris, his public appeal to Executive Branch workers — over the head of the President — to provide information to him exclusively of "graft, corruption, communists and treason" in the Administration.

While McCarthy was certainly not the first American to take an audacious step beyond the limit of his authority and good sense — Aaron Burr's challenge of a duel to Alexander Hamilton and General George McClellan's reference to President Abraham Lincoln as a "baboon," come to mind — McCarthy's arrogance was certainly on a par with all of the known historical precedents.

His solicitation to Administration employees to become whistle blowers had riveted Ike's attention on the Committee's hearings with the Army, as never before. He directed his closest lieutenants on May 28, 1954 to make sure that all of the Senators on the McCarthy Committee were made aware that the Administration was keeping an eye on everything that was going on during the hearings. They were warned that they couldn't "pull a fast one" without Ike's hearing about it.[171]

EISENHOWER'S COLUMBIA SPEECH, MAY 13, 1954

A combative Ike worked for a good part of Sunday, May 30, 1954, on his speech to be delivered the next day at the Columbia Bi-Centennial Dinner. Jim Hagerty, on the other hand, took a day away from the White House in an attempt to relax at home. The job of being press secretary, however, required him to be on call seven days a week, twenty-four hours a day. By noon the President had

---

[171] Hagerty White House Minutes, Id., 5/28/54.

already called him several times. Ike was concerned that the portion of the speech which announced the Executive Branch's compelling need to protect "the nation's vital secrets" was too narrow. He told Hagerty that this was an invitation to McCarthy to circumvent the mandate by labeling his demands for documents and testimony as unrelated to national secrets. Ike, therefore, wanted the second paragraph on Page 6 of the speech broadened to prohibit as well, disclosure of matters involving "the nation's obvious interests."[172]

The second phone call from the President to Hagerty on that Sunday morning included a direction to insert a clause into the speech slamming McCarthy hard for his violation of the constitutional principle of the separation of the powers and prerogatives of the three branches of government. Eisenhower's ire over what he saw as McCarthy's attempt to trespass on the turf of the Executive Branch was at its all-time peak: "I'm going to make this a finished fight with McCarthy. I'm going to the people with it."[173]

Inspired by the President's verve and determination, Hagerty arrived at the White House at 8:15 on Monday morning. Perhaps tired from the previous day's work on the Columbia speech, the President did not arrive until 9:00 a.m. But once settled into the Oval Office, he and Hagerty wasted no time. They immediately began work on several changes to the speech. In addition to expanding the Chief Executive's mandate to hold private, matters involving the "nation's obvious interests," the President, to Hagerty's mild surprise, inserted two paragraphs attacking "any individual who because they differ with us, classified other individuals or parties as treasonous."[174] The President also decided to leave in his speech "all remarks aimed at McCarthy, particularly those dealing with 'demagogues'."[175]

The President delivered the speech at noon. No sooner had he left the rostrum when the wire services immediately contacted Hagerty seeking to get him to say that President Eisenhower was specifically

---

[172] Id., 5/30/54.
[173] Id.
[174] Id., 5/31/54.
[175] Id.

talking about McCarthy. Hagerty "refused to interpret the President's speech and let it go at that."[176]

Eisenhower's Columbia University speech was a smash hit. He was interrupted twenty five times by enthusiastic applause — the majority of the spurts of applause coming after portions of the talk dealing with McCarthy. Again McCarthy was not mentioned by name but there was no doubt in the room as to whom the President was referring.

At Hagerty's table there was, among several others, William Paley, the President of CBS. After the speech, Paley pulled Hagerty aside to tell him that he was going back to his office and order "all his newscasters on radio and television to plug the speech."[177]

Ike was elated. The reception the speech received was beyond all expectations. Because the audience consisted of mostly academics, he had anticipated a muted reaction. The tumultuous ring of approval was an extremely pleasant surprise. Once back in Washington the President expressed extreme satisfaction with how things had gone to his staff.

Eisenhower's bold declaration of policy that members of his staff have no political existence apart from himself and no legislative responsibility such as that imposed by Congress on some Department heads, had effectively squelched McCarthy's offensive against the Administration. With military-like authoritarianism Ike had placed his people in the same position as staff officers in a military organization, whose duties consisted of advising and counseling, not deciding issues.

Faced with a stone wall at the other end of Pennsylvania Avenue, McCarthy was forced to switch gears and find new targets. But Ike was unrelenting. His bitter but diffuse experiences with McCarthy had galvanized into a rock-solid conviction that McCarthy had gotten way out of line and was now an enemy who had to be defeated and demolished.

---

[176] Id.
[177] Id., 5/31/54.

TRAPPED IN A PIT

Back in the Senate Caucus room, a cross-fire of mutual recriminations continued. But without McCarthy's ability to put Eisenhower Administration officials on the stand, the hearing began to degenerate into a tawdry affair with many of the earmarks of a messy divorce trial.

The trial lawyer Roy Cohn would eventually become would have thrived in such a bare-knuckles fight. But the Cohn of 1954 was too personally involved to be effective. To Army Counsel, John G. Adams, Cohn threatened "to wreck the Army". Large parts of the hearings were about the Cohn-Schine relationship in which Cohn *was* the main story. As for McCarthy, he could have taken a back seat and let Cohn be the whipping boy, thereby deflecting attention away from himself. But had he been disposed to do that, he wouldn't have been Joe McCarthy. Such calculated scapegoating, a daily occurrence in image-obsessed D.C., was not McCarthy's style. The man seemed preternaturally incapable of shedding the limelight, as he peppered the proceedings with frequent and endless refrains of "point of order" and snide insinuations.

THE PHOTOGRAPH

During the hearings, Roy Cohn- officially Chief Counsel to the Committee but in reality McCarthy's man all the way — introduced into evidence a photograph depicting Private G. David Schine standing next to Secretary of the Army, Robert Stevens. The photo appeared to be of the two of them alone. Both Cohn and Schine eventually took the witness stand. Each of them testified that the photograph had been requested by Stevens and that no other persons had been cropped out of the picture. As introduced, the picture was a powerful piece of evidence. The Army's contention that McCarthy and his minions had pressed hard for special treatment for Schine would be seriously undercut by a photograph requested by the Secretary of the Army of just he and Schine.

But, the wily Joseph Welch, special counsel to the Army, had a surprise in store for the McCarthy people. Possessed of a folksy charm and a disarmingly gentle way about him, nobody was better than Joseph N. Welch at seizing ownership of the moment. And it was in such a moment that Welch stunned the panel, witnesses and gallery alike — not to mention McCarthy and Cohn — by introducing as a hearing exhibit a wider shot of Schine and Stevens. This one showed that Cohn and Schine had testified falsely because appearing next to them in the picture was McGuire Air Force Base Wing Commander, Colonel Jack Bradley, standing to Schine's right. A fourth man, standing to the right of Bradley had only his sleeve in the picture, but was later identified as Frank Carr, another McCarthy aide.

Welch squeezed the dramatic moment for all it was worth. Throughout the entire hearing there had been a strong undercurrent of homosexuality in the proceedings, cast as an additional inquiry into the possible security risk of homosexuals in sensitive government positions. The issue had been brought up on occasions prior to the incident of the allegedly doctored photograph. From the beginning Welch had unrelentingly gay-baited Roy Cohn and was largely responsible for creating the sub plot of the hearings, i.e. the suggestion that Cohn was in a homosexual relationship with Schine. Such a relationship was implied only but there was no mistaking the implication, which had been crafted by a skilled litigator, and permeated the hearings.

Welch seemed to be trying to embarrass McCarthy — perhaps as pay-back for his harsh attacks on the Army — and seized the opportunity to play the homosexuality card again during his questioning of McCarthy staff member, James Juliana, as to the origins of the photograph. The following exchange — pointed as it was — provided some comic relief from the tension of the proceedings:

Joseph Welch (questioning James Juliana): "Did you think this (the photo) came from a pixie?"

At this point McCarthy asked that the question be re-read.

Senator McCarthy: "Will Counsel (i.e. Welch) for my benefit define — I think he might be an expert on that — what a pixie is."

Mr. Welch: "Yes, I should say, Mr. Senator, that a pixie is a close relative to a fairy (laughter from the Chambers). Shall I proceed sir? Have I enlightened you?"

Senator McCarthy: "As I said, I think you may be an authority on what a pixie is."[178]

THE HOOVER LETTER

During the Truman Administration and the early months of the Eisenhower Administration, J. Edgar Hoover, the Director of the FBI, was a staunch supporter of Joseph McCarthy — viewing him as a kindred spirit and staunch ally in the war against Communism. But Hoover's enthusiasm for McCarthy began to wane as the latter, a reputed alcoholic, raged against the CIA and then the United States Army. By the time the Army-McCarthy Hearings began in earnest in May of 1954, Hoover had soured on his erstwhile ally. McCarthy had become an embarrassment to him and he did not wish the Bureau and his own legacy to be tainted by McCarthy's extreme tactics. Such was the backdrop for the next significant incident.

After the photograph was discredited, McCarthy was desperate to reverse the momentum which was clearly turning against him. Needing a quick and decisive tactical victory, McCarthy produced a copy of a confidential letter he claimed was written and signed in January 1951 by J. Edgar Hoover. The purported letter was addressed to United States Army Intelligence warning of subversives in the Army Signal Corps.

The McCarthy group saw a dual benefit in the introduction of the letter: First there was the sensationalism of the head-line grabbing accusation against the Army of subversion in the Signal Corps. Second — and equally important — was McCarthy's claim that the letter was in the Army's files when Robert Stevens assumed his position as Secretary in 1953. Stevens was further accused of having

---

[178] Point of Order", Emile D. Antonio (Documentary Film, 1964).

willfully ignored the letter, an allegation which if true, would have implications of traitorous conduct.

The always astute and resourceful Joseph Welch was not easily hoodwinked. He immediately challenged the validity and authenticity of the letter by alleging that McCarthy's copy absolutely did not come from the FBI's files.

McCarthy quickly admitted that he did not receive the letter from the FBI but still strongly stood behind its authenticity.

Welch bided his time until McCarthy took the stand to testify. Direct testimony from McCarthy was elicited under oath by Senate Committee attorney, Ray Jenkins, endorsing the authenticity of the purported letter. Then it was Welch's turn to cross-examine. Welch got McCarthy to admit that the document had been given to him by an intelligence officer. When pressed for details, however, he refused to identify his source.

Welch had McCarthy perfectly set up for what came next. He called to the stand as a rebuttal witness, Robert Collier, an assistant to Senate Counsel Jenkins, who read a letter from Attorney General Herbert Brownell, under whose jurisdiction the FBI fell. Brownell stated in his letter that Hoover had examined the purported letter and reported back that no such copy existed in the FBI's files. Hoover further stated that he neither wrote nor ordered the letter to be written. The inference that McCarthy or someone on his team had manufactured evidence was unmistakable — bolstered by McCarthy's reputation for leveling charges based on spurious evidence.

That the demurrer had come from Brownell, a member of Ike's cabinet and an Eisenhower loyalist, led participants and observers alike to conclude that the President had once again come to the aid of his beloved Army by helping the anti-McCarthy forces in an important way. Eisenhower's continuing influence on the hearings was the elephant in the room that no one overtly acknowledged. Even more devastating to McCarthy's cause was that his former ally, J. Edgar Hoover, had unceremoniously dumped him.

Joe McCarthy had overplayed his hand. He began to drink more heavily than ever.[179] The hearings were now clearly going against him. Desperate times called for desperate measures and Joseph McCarthy was more than ready to employ them.

COUP DE GRÁS

As is not unusual with both judicial and legislative hearings, the principals of the Army-McCarthy hearings met privately before they got under way. There were sensitive matters which both sides just as soon preferred be kept out of the hearings because they were prejudicial to one side or the other, without having any essential substantive value.

The McCarthy team was anxious to ensure that Roy Cohn's sexual preferences be kept out of the proceedings and that the nature of the relationship between Cohn and Schine also be out of bounds.

The Army's lawyers on the other hand wanted the former affiliation of Fred Fisher, a member of Welch's Boston law firm, with the National Lawyer's Guild (NLG), to also be withheld from public airing during the televised hearings. The NLG was a group which had been called "the legal bulwark of the Communist Party"[180] by no less than Herbert Brownell, Eisenhower's Attorney General.

Welch had included Fred Fisher on his legal team for the Army-McCarthy Hearings. But well before the hearings began, Welch confirmed Fisher's former membership in the National Lawyer's Guild and confronted him. Fisher readily admitted his membership, whereupon Welch promptly dispatched him back to Boston. Fisher was replaced on Welch's hearing staff by another attorney. The substitution of the new staff attorney for Fred Fisher was reported in the New York Times.[181]

---

[179] The Fifties, Id., p. 252.
[180] Anatomy of a Counter-Bar Association: The Chicago Counsel of Lawyers, by Michael Powell (28 July 2006).
[181] New York Times, April 16, 1954.

Before the hearings began Cohn and Welch agreed that in return
for there being no mention of Fisher's NLG affiliation, there would
likewise be no explicit mention of Cohn's reputed homosexuality.

When the climactic exchange of the Army-McCarthy Hearings
occurred on June 9, 1954, the aforementioned backdrop was not
generally known. The June 9th events, as reported by the official
stenographer, appear as follows in the transcript of the hearings:[182]

> Secretary STEVENS. Gentlemen of the
> committee, I am here today at the request of
> this committee. You have my assurance of the
> fullest cooperation.
>
> In order that we may all be quite clear as to just
> why this hearing has come about, it is
> necessary for me to refer at the outset to Pvt. G.
> David Schine, a former consultant of this
> committee. David Schine was eligible for the
> draft. Efforts were made by the chairman of
> this committee, Senator Joseph R. McCarthy,
> and the subcommittee's chief counsel, Mr. Roy
> M. Cohn, to secure a commission for him. Mr.
> Schine was not qualified, and he was not
> commissioned. Selective service then drafted
> him. Subsequent efforts were made to seek
> preferential treatment for him after he was
> inducted.
>
> Before getting into the Schine story I want to
> make two general comments.
>
> First, it is my responsibility to speak for the
> Army. The Army is about a million and a half
> men and women, in posts across this country
> and around the world, on active duty and in the
> National Guard and Organized Reserves, plus

[182] The Army-McCarthy Hearings, 1954, by Robert D. Marcus and Anthony
Marcus, eds (St. James, New York, Brandywine Press, 1998).

hundreds of thousands of loyal and faithful civil servants.

Senator MCCARTHY. Mr. Chairman, a point of order.

Senator MUNDT. Senator McCarthy has a point of order.

Senator MCCARTHY. Mr. Stevens is not speaking for the Army. He is speaking for Mr. Stevens, for Mr. Adams, and Mr. Hensel. The committee did not make the Army a party to this controversy, and I think it is highly improper to try to make the Army a party. Mr. Stevens can only speak for himself. . . .

All we were investigating has been some Communists in the Army, a very small percentage, I would say much less than 1 percent. And when the Secretary says that, in effect "I am speaking for the Army," he is putting the 99.9 percent of good, honorable, loyal men in the Army into the position of trying to oppose the exposure of Communists in the Army.

I think it should be made clear at the outset, so we need not waste time on it, hour after hour, that Mr. Stevens is speaking for Mr. Stevens and those who are speaking through him; when Mr. Adams speaks, he is speaking for Mr. Adams and those who are speaking through him, and likewise Mr. Hensel.

I may say I resent very, very much this attempt to connect the great American Army with this attempt to sabotage the efforts of this committee's investigation into communism. . . .

****

Mr. ADAMS. About that time these two friends left, and because I wanted Senator McCarthy to restate before Mr. Cohn what he had told me on the courthouse steps, I said, "Let's talk about Schine."

That started a chain of events, an experience similar to none which I have had in my life.

Mr. Cohn became extremely agitated, became extremely abusive. He cursed me and then Senator McCarthy. The abuse went in waves. He would be very abusive and then it would kind of abate and things would be friendly for a few moments. Everybody would eat a little bit more, and then it would start in again. It just kept on.

I was trying to catch a 1:30 train, but Mr. Cohn was so violent by then that I felt I had better not do it and leave him that angry with me and that angry with Senator McCarthy because of a remark I had made. So I stayed and missed my 1:30 train. I thought surely I would be able to get out of there by 2:30. The luncheon concluded.

Mr. JENKINS. You say you were afraid to leave Senator McCarthy alone there with him? Mr. Adams, what did he say? You say he was very abusive.

Mr. ADAMS. He was extremely abusive.

Mr. JENKINS. Was or not any obscene language used?

Mr. ADAMS. Yes.

Mr. JENKINS. Just omit that and tell what he did say which constituted abuse, in your opinion.

Mr. ADAMS. I have stated before, sir, the tone of voice has as much to do with abuse as words. I do not remember the phrases, I do not remember the sentences, but I do remember the violence.

Mr. JENKINS. Do you remember the subject?

Mr. ADAMS. The subject was Schine. The subject was the fact—the thing that Cohn was angry about, the thing that he was so violent about, was the fact that, (1), the Army was not agreeing to an assignment for Schine and, (2), that Senator McCarthy was not supporting his staff in its efforts to get Schine assigned to New York. So his abuse was directed partly to me and partly to Senator McCarthy.

As I say, it kind of came in waves. There would be a period of extreme abuse, and then there would be a period where it would get almost back to normal, and ice cream would be ordered, and then about halfway through that a little more of the same. I missed the 2:30 train, also.

This violence continued. It was a remarkable thing. At first Senator McCarthy seemed to be trying to conciliate. He seemed to be trying to conciliate Cohn and not to state anything contrary to what he had stated to me in the morning. But then he more or less lapsed into silence. . . .

So I went down to room 101. Mr. Cohn was there and Mr. Carr was there. As I remember, we lunched together in the Senate cafeteria, and everything was peaceful. When we returned to room 101, toward the latter part of the conversation I asked Cohn—I knew that 90 percent of all inductees ultimately face overseas duty and I knew that one day we were going to face that problem with Mr. Cohn as to Schine.

So I thought I would lay a little groundwork for future trouble I guess. I asked him what would happen if Schine got overseas duty.

Mr. JENKINS. You mean you were breaking the news gently, Mr. Adams?

Mr. ADAMS. Yes, sir; that is right. I asked him what would happen if Schine got overseas duty. He responded with vigor and force, "Stevens is through as Secretary of the Army."

I said, "Oh, Roy," something to this effect, "Oh, Roy, don't say that. Come on. Really, what is going to happen if Schine gets overseas duty?"

He responded with even more force, "We will wreck the Army."

Then he said, "The first thing we are going to do is get General Ryan for the way he has treated Dave at Fort Dix. Dave gets through at Fort Dix tomorrow or this week, and as soon as he is gone we are going to get General Ryan for the obscene way in which he has permitted Schine to be treated up there."

He said, "We are not going to do it ourselves. We have another committee of the Congress interested in it."

Then he said, "I wouldn't put it past you to do this. We will start investigations. We have enough stuff on the Army to keep investigations going indefinitely, and if anything like such-and-such doublecross occurs, that is what we will do."

This remark was not to be taken lightly in the context in which it was given to me. . . .

****

Mr. JENKINS. You will recall, Mr. Cohn, that he testified that you said that if Schine went overseas, Stevens was through as Secretary of the Army?

Mr. COHN. I heard him say that, sir.

Mr. JENKINS. Did you or not?

Mr. COHN. No, sir.

Mr. JENKINS. Did you say anything like that, Mr. Cohn?

Mr. COHN. No, sir, and my recollection is that I did not. I have talked to Mr. Carr who was sitting there the whole time, and he says I did not. . . .

Mr. JENKINS. All right, now you are saying you did not say it, Mr. Cohn?

Mr. COHN. Yes, sir. I am saying I am sure I did not make that statement, and I am sure that Mr. Adams and anybody else with any sense, and Mr. Adams has a lot of sense, could ever believe that I was threatening to wreck the Army or that I could wreck the Army. I say, sir, that the statement is ridiculous.

Mr. JENKINS. I am talking about Stevens being through as Secretary of the Army.

Mr. COHN. That is equally ridiculous, sir.

Mr. JENKINS. And untrue?

Mr. COHN. Yes, sir, equally ridiculous and untrue, I could not cause the President of the United States to remove Stevens as Secretary of the Army. . . .

Mr. WELCH. Mr. Cohn, what is the exact number of Communists or subversives that are loose today in these defense plants?

Mr. COHN. The exact number that is loose, sir?

Mr. WELCH. Yes, sir.

Mr. COHN. I don't know.

Mr. WELCH. Roughly how many?

Mr. COHN. I can only tell you, sir, what we know about it.

Mr. WELCH. That is 130, is that right?

Mr. COHN. Yes, sir. I am going to try to particularize for you, if I can.

Mr. WELCH. I am in a hurry. I don't want the sun to go down while they are still in there, if we can get them out.

Mr. COHN. I am afraid we won't be able to work that fast, sir.

Mr. WELCH. I have a suggestion about it, sir. How many are there?

Mr. COHN. I believe the figure is approximately 130.

Mr. WELCH. Approximately one-two-three?

Mr. COHN. Yes, sir. Those are people, Mr. Welch—

Mr. WELCH. I don't care. You told us who they are. In how many plants are they?

Mr. COHN. How many plants?

Mr. WELCH. How many plants.

Mr. COHN. Yes, sir; just I minute, sir. I see 16 offhand, sir.

Mr. WELCH. Sixteen plants?

Mr. COHN. Yes, sir.

Mr. WELCH. Where are they, sir?

Mr. COHN. Senator McCarthy—

Mr. WELCH. Reel off the cities.

Mr. COHN. Would you stop me if I am going too far?

Mr. WELCH. You can't go too far revealing Communists, Mr. Cohn. Reel off the cities for us.

Mr. COHN. Schenectady, N.Y.; Syracuse, N.Y.; Rome, N.Y.; Quincy, Mass.; Fitchburg, Mass.; Buffalo, N.Y.; Dunkirk, N.Y.; another at Buffalo, N.Y.; Cambridge, Mass.; New Bedford, Mass.; Boston, Mass.; Quincy, Mass.; Lynn, Mass.; Pittsfield Mass.; Boston, Mass.

Mr. WELCH. Mr. Cohn, you not only frighten me, you make me ashamed when there are so many in Massachusetts. [Laughter.] This is not a laughing matter, believe me. Are you alarmed at that situation, Mr. Cohn?

Mr. COHN. Yes, sir; I am.

Mr. WELCH. Nothing could be more alarming, could it?

Mr. COHN. It certainly is a very alarming thing.

Mr. WELCH. Will you not, before the sun goes down, give those names to the FBI and at least have those men put under surveillance.

Mr. COHN. Mr. Welch, the FBI—

Senator MCCARTHY. Mr. Chairman.

Mr. WELCH. That is a fair question.

Senator MCCARTHY. Mr. Chairman, let's not be ridiculous. Mr. Welch knows, as I have told him a dozen times, that the FBI has all of this information. The defense plants have the information. The only thing we can do is to try and publicly expose these individuals and hope that they will be gotten rid of. And you know that, Mr. Welch.

Mr. WELCH. I do not know that. . . .

Cannot the FBI put these 130 men under surveillance before sundown tomorrow?

Mr. COHN. Sir, if there is need for surveillance in the case of espionage or anything like that, I can well assure you that Mr. John Edgar Hoover and his men know a lot better than I, and I quite respectfully suggest, sir, than probably a lot of us, just who should be put under surveillance. I do not propose to tell the FBI how to run its shop. It does it very well.

Mr. WELCH. And they do it, don't they, Mr. Cohn?

Mr. COHN. When the need arises, of course.

Mr. WELCH. And will you tell them tonight, Mr. Cohn, that here is a case where the need has arisen, so that it can be done by sundown tomorrow night?

Mr. COHN. No, sir; there is no need for my telling the FBI what to do about this or anything else. . . .

Mr. WELCH. Mr. Cohn, tell me once more: Every time you learn of a Communist or a spy anywhere, is it your policy to get them out as fast as possible?

Mr. COHN. Surely, we want them out as fast as possible, sir.

Mr. WELCH. And whenever you learn of one from now on, Mr. Cohn, I beg of you, will you tell somebody about them quick?

Mr. COHN. Mr. Welch, with great respect, I work for the committee here. They know how we go about handling situations of Communist infiltration and failure to act on FBI information about Communist infiltration. If they are displeased with the speed with which I and the group of men who work with me proceed, if they are displeased with the order in which we move, I am sure they will give me appropriate instructions along those lines, and I will follow any which they give me.

Mr. WELCH. May I add my small voice, sir, and say whenever you know about a subversive or a Communist spy, please hurry. Will you remember those words?

Senator MCCARTHY. Mr. Chairman.

Mr. COHN. Mr. Welch, I can assure you, sir, as far as I am concerned, and certainly as far as the chairman of this committee and the members, and the members of the staff, are concerned, we are a small group, but we proceed as expeditiously as is humanly possible to get out Communists and traitors and to bring to light the mechanism by which they have been permitted to remain where they were for so long a period of time.

Senator MCCARTHY. Mr. Chairman, in view of that question—

Senator MUNDT. Have you a point of order?

Senator MCCARTHY. Not exactly, Mr. Chairman, but in view of Mr. Welch's request that the information be given once we know of anyone who might be performing any work for the Communist Party, I think we should tell him that he has in his law firm a young man named Fisher whom he recommended, incidentally, to do work on this committee, who has been for a number of years a member of an organization which was named, oh, years and years ago, as the legal bulwark of the Communist Party, an organization which always swings to the defense of anyone who dares to expose Communists. I certainly assume that Mr. Welch did not know of this young man at the time he recommended him as the assistant counsel for this committee, but he has such terror and such a great desire to know where anyone is located who may be serving the Communist cause, Mr. Welch, that I thought we should just call to your attention the fact that your Mr. Fisher, who is still in your law firm today, whom you asked to have down here looking over the secret and classified material, is a member of an organization, not named by me but named by various committees, named by the Attorney General, as I recall, and I think I quote this verbatim, as "the legal bulwark of the Communist Party."

He belonged to that for a sizable number of years, according to his own admission, and he belonged to it long after it had been exposed as the legal arm of the Communist Party.

Knowing that, Mr. Welch, I just felt that I had a duty to respond to your urgent request that before sundown, when we know of anyone serving the Communist cause, we let the agency know. We are now letting you know that your man did belong to this organization for, either 3 or 4 years, belonged to it long after he was out of law school.

I don't think you can find anyplace, anywhere, an organization which has done more to defend Communists—I am again quoting the report— to defend Communists, to defend espionage agents, and to aid the Communist cause, than the man whom you originally wanted down here at your right hand instead of Mr. St. Clair.

I have hesitated bringing that up, but I have been rather bored with your phony requests to Mr. Cohn here that he personally get every Communist out of government before sundown. Therefore, we will give you information about the young man in your own organization.

I am not asking you at this time to explain why you tried to foist him on this committee. Whether you knew he was a member of that Communist organization or not, I don't know. I assume you did not, Mr. Welch, because I get the impression that, while you are quite an actor, you play for a laugh, I don't think you have any conception of the danger of the Communist Party. I don't think you yourself would ever knowingly aid the Communist cause. I think you are unknowingly aiding it when you try to burlesque this hearing in which we are attempting to bring out the facts, however.

Mr. WELCH. Mr. Chairman.

Senator MUNDT. Mr. Welch, the Chair should say he has no recognition or no memory of Mr. Welch's recommending either Mr. Fisher or anybody else as counsel for this committee.

I will recognize Mr. Welch.

Senator MCCARTHY. Mr. Chairman, I will give you the news story on that.

Mr. WELCH. Mr. Chairman, under these circumstances I must have something approaching a personal privilege.

Senator MUNDT. You may have it, sir. It will not be taken out of your time.

Mr. WELCH. Senator McCarthy, I did not know—Senator, sometimes you say "May I have your attention?"

Senator MCCARTHY. I am listening to you. I can listen with one ear.

Mr. WELCH. This time I want you to listen with both.

Senator MCCARTHY. Yes.

Mr. WELCH. Senator McCarthy, I think until this moment—

Senator MCCARTHY. Jim, will you get the news story to the effect that this man belonged to this Communist-front organization? Will you get the citations showing that this was the legal arm of the Communist Party, and the length of time that he belonged, and the fact that he was recommended by Mr. Welch? I think that should be in the record.

Mr. WELCH. You won't need anything in the record when I have finished telling you this.

Until this moment, Senator, I think I never really gauged your cruelty or your recklessness. Fred Fisher is a young man who went to the Harvard Law School and came into my firm and is starting what looks to be a brilliant career with us.

When I decided to work for this committee I asked Jim St. Clair, who sits on my right, to be my first assistant. I said to Jim, "Pick somebody in the firm who works under you that you would like." He chose Fred Fisher and they came down on an afternoon plane. That night, when he had taken a little stab at trying to see what the case was about, Fred Fisher and Jim St. Clair and I went to dinner together. I then said to these two young men, "Boys, I don't know anything about you except I have always liked you, but if there is anything funny in the life of either one of you that would hurt anybody in this case you speak up quick."

Fred Fisher said, "Mr. Welch, when I was in law school and for a period of months after, I belonged to the Lawyers Guild," as you have suggested, Senator. He went on to say, "I am secretary of the Young Republicans League in Newton with the son of Massachusetts' Governor, and I have the respect and admiration of the 25 lawyers or so in Hale & Dorr."

I said, "Fred, I just don't think I am going to ask you to work on the case. If I do, one of these days that will come out and go over national television and it will just hurt like the dickens."

So, Senator, I asked him to go back to Boston.

Little did I dream you could be so reckless and cruel as to do an injury to that lad. It is true he is still with Hale & Dorr. It is true that he will continue to be with Hale & Dorr. It is, I regret to say, equally true that I fear he shall always bear a scar needlessly inflicted by you. If it were in my power to forgive you for your reckless cruelty, I will do so. I like to think I am a gentleman, but your forgiveness will have to come from someone other than me.

Senator MCCARTHY. Mr. Chairman.

Senator MUNDT. Senator McCarthy?

Senator MCCARTHY. May I say that Mr. Welch talks about this being cruel and reckless. He was just baiting; he has been baiting Mr. Cohn here for hours, requesting that Mr. Cohn, before sundown, get out of any department of Government anyone who is serving the Communist cause.

I just give this man's record, and I want to say, Mr. Welch, that it has been labeled long before he became a member, as early as 1944—

Mr. WELCH. Senator, may we not drop this? We know he belonged to the Lawyers Guild, and Mr. Cohn nods his head at me. I did you, I think, no personal injury, Mr. Cohn.

Mr. COHN. No, sir.

Mr. WELCH. I meant to do you no personal injury, and if I did, beg your pardon.

Let us not assassinate this lad further, Senator. You have done enough. Have you no sense of decency sir, at long last? Have you left no sense of decency?

Senator MCCARTHY. I know this hurts you, Mr. Welch. But I may say, Mr. Chairman, on a point of personal privilege, and I would like to finish it—

Mr. WELCH. Senator, I think it hurts you, too, sir.

Senator MCCARTHY. I would like to finish this.

Mr. Welch has been filibustering this hearing, he has been talking day after day about how he wants to get anyone tainted with communism out before sundown. I know Mr. Cohn would rather not have me go into this. I intend to, however, Mr. Welch talks about any sense of decency. If I say anything which is not the truth, then I would like to know about it.

The foremost legal bulwark of the Communist Party, its front organizations, and controlled unions, and which, since its inception, has never failed to rally to the legal defense of the Communist Party, and individual members thereof, including known espionage agents.

Now, that is not the language of Senator McCarthy. That is the language of the Un-American Activities Committee. And I can go on with many more citations. It seems that Mr. Welch is pained so deeply he thinks it is improper for me to give the record, the

Communist front record, of the man whom he wanted to foist upon this committee. But it doesn't pain him at all—there is no pain in his chest about the unfounded charges against Mr. Frank Carr; there is no pain there about the attempt to destroy the reputation and take the jobs away from the young men who were working in my committee.

And, Mr. Welch, if I have said anything here which is untrue, then tell me. I have heard you and everyone else talk so much about laying the truth upon the table that when I hear—and it is completely phony, Mr. Welch, I have listened to you for a long time—when you say "Now, before sundown, you must get these people out of Government," I want to have it very clear, very clear that you were not so serious about that when you tried to recommend this man for this committee.

And may I say, Mr. Welch, in fairness to you, I have reason to believe that you did not know about his Communist-front record at the time you recommended him. I don't think you would have recommended him to the committee, if you knew that.

I think it is entirely possible you learned that after you recommended him.

Senator MUNDT. The Chair would like to say again that he does not believe that Mr. Welch recommended Mr. Fisher as counsel for this committee, because he has through his office all the recommendations that were made. He does not recall any that came from Mr. Welch, and that would include Mr. Fisher.

Senator MCCARTHY. Let me ask Mr. Welch. You brought him down, did you not, to act as your assistant?

Mr. WELCH. Mr. McCarthy, I will not discuss this with you further. You have sat within 6 feet of me, and could have asked me about Fred Fisher. You have brought it out. If there is a God in heaven, it will do neither you nor your cause any good. I will not discuss it further. I will not ask Mr. Cohn any more questions. You, Mr. Chairman, may, if you will, call the next witness.

Senator MUNDT. Are there any questions?

Mr. JENKINS. No further questions, Mr. Chairman.

Mr. JENKINS. Senator McCarthy, how do you regard the communistic threat to our Government as compared with other threats with which it is confronted?

Senator MCCARTHY. Mr. Jenkins, the thing that I think we must remember is that this is a war which a brutalitarian force has won to a greater extent than any brutalitarian force has won a war in the history of the world before.

For example, Christianity, which has been in existence for 2,000 years, has not converted, convinced nearly as many people as this Communist brutalitarianism has enslaved in 106 years, and they are not going to stop.

I know that many of my good friends seem to feel that this is a sort of a game you can play, that you can talk about communism as though it is something 10,000 miles away.

Mr. Jenkins, in answer to your question, let me say it is right here with us now. Unless we make sure that there is no infiltration of our Government, then just as certain as you sit there, in the period of our lives you will see a red world. There is no question about that, Mr. Jenkins. . . ."

Following this bitter and emotional confrontation between McCarthy and Welch, the latter left the hearing room and removed himself from further participation in the hearings. As he left the Caucus Room, however, he managed to get in a parting shot:

"You have seen fit to bring (the affair) out and if there is a God n Heaven, it will do neither you nor your cause any good!"

Welch then yielded to Acting Chair, Senator Karl Mundt, to call the next witness.

As Welch rose to leave, the gallery met his departure with a loud burst of applause. An uncomprehending McCarthy turned to Roy Cohn, and in a state of shock asked his chief counsel, "What happened?" It is not known what Cohn's response, if any, was; but it would not have been inaccurate had he replied, "You just got shot down on nationwide T.V. and your career is over."

Although the televised hearings dragged on for another week, the high water mark of the drama was reached on June 9, 1954. Everything after that was anti-climactic. Various theories were advanced to explain McCarthy's meltdown. In the electronic media a popular opinion was that he had been a hot personality in a cool medium and the contrast did not serve him well. Others blamed his heavy drinking for his downfall.

Still others opined that McCarthy had already been deeply wounded by the Murrow broadcasts and the more subtle campaign waged by the Eisenhower Administration against McCarthyism. Thus, the hearings merely confirmed for millions in the viewing public the negative perception of McCarthy already gathering currency. This theory, however, seems to fail to come to grips with just how boorish, clownish and bullying McCarthy had come across on television. The man seemed devoid of empathy and the public, in turn, had little empathy with him.

Whatever the explanation for McCarthy's sudden and dramatic implosion, it seems to have been the product of a self-inflicted wound. For the remainder of the hearings, McCarthy continued to rail against communism and subversion in defense plants, the CIA, the Army and various other government departments and agencies, all the while over-using the phrase, "Point of Order." Perhaps more than any other, the reaction he most often elicited was boredom.

FALL-OUT

As the hearings wound down, nerves began to fray and verbal altercations occurred with greater frequency. The most noteworthy of the sparring matches took place between Senator Joseph McCarthy and Senator Stuart Symington (D. Missouri). Prior to the hearings both men had presidential ambitions. McCarthy's reputation had been smashed to bits by the hearings, although it is not clear that he knew it; but Symington's ambitions were still intact in the summer of 1954. A handsome, forceful and well-spoken man from a border state, Symington now saw his stock as a possible candidate for president, rise steadily. The Democratic Party ultimately spurned Symington's overtures to be nominated for President, by turning to Adlai Stevenson again in 1956 and to John F. Kennedy in 1960. Of course, Symington had no way of knowing that in 1954, and a verbal spat with a fading Joe McCarthy could only in his mind help his image among fellow Democrats.

The context for the loud and public confrontation between the two men was the power which McCarthy continued to wield over the Investigations Subcommittee, despite Senator Mundt's nominal and temporary chairmanship during the hearings. The committee staff were still mainly men chosen by McCarthy, whose loyalties were exclusively to him. Democrats on the Committee had long been frustrated by their difficulty in gaining access to committee files and to the outright denial of access to a number of files labeled "secret".

Towards the end of the hearings, Symington began to hint that some members of McCarthy's own staff might themselves be subversives, and that the evidence was in the so-called "secret files". Republican members protested that Symington's insinuations were meaningless because he had provided no detail.

Symington, itching for a fight, offered to take the stand and name names but only if McCarthy would sign an agreement to investigate his own staff.

Tempers flared — McCarthy adamantly refused Symington's offer, calling him "Sanctimonious Stu" and labeling his accusations an "unfounded smear". He further held that the agreement presented for his signature contained false statements designed to smear his men. For this he rebuked Symington by stating, "You're not fooling anyone." Symington's immediate retort was "Senator, the American people have had a look at you now for six weeks; you're not fooling anyone, either."[183]

Symington's words turned out to be prophetic. By the end of June, 1954, the Gallup Poll reported 45% of Americans disapproving of McCarthy and his methods, with only 54% approving. In only six months, McCarthy's popularity with the American public had completely reversed itself.

THE VERDICTS

Senator McCarthy was acquitted of any wrongdoing in the Schine case by the Senate Subcommittee on Investigations — though not in the court of public opinion. The members of the Committee were unable to find sufficient evidence that McCarthy himself exercised improper influence on behalf of G. David Schine. Not so with Roy Cohn who the Committee found had engaged in "unduly or aggressive efforts" to gain special treatment for Schine.

The Army was not completely exonerated of wrongdoing either. The Committee found that Secretary Stevens and Army Counsel Adams "made efforts to terminate or influence the investigations and hearings at Fort Monmouth." Adams was also found to have

---

[183] Not Without Honor: The History of American Anti-Communism, Richard Gid Powers, (Yale University Press, 1998), p. 271.

made vigorous and diligent efforts to block subpoenas for members of the Army Loyalty and Screening Board "by means of personal appeals to certain members of the (McCarthy) Committee."

After 36 days of hearings and the testimony of 32 witnesses, who uttered two million words from the witness stand, the actual findings were indecisive and ambivalent; leading each of the two polarized camps to claim victory. The American public little noted the official results. They were sophisticated enough to know that any findings or verdicts would of necessity reflect the split on the Committee between Republicans and Democrats. In short, it was too politicized to be objective.

PART III – THE FALL

CHAPTER TEN

Censure

The official verdicts in the hearings had little to do with Joseph McCarthy's eventual fate. Winning or losing in a politically-charged battle is an elusive concept. The real results are found in the aftermath.

One sign of how the aftermath would play out was the resignation of Roy M. Cohn as Chief Counsel to the Committee before the official findings were even released. Cohn had been Joe McCarthy's alter ego in many ways — the action side of his personality — the man who would synthesize McCarthy's broadside attacks into specific steps designed to implement his ideas and notions.

The loss of Cohn under such inglorious circumstances was at once a major defeat for McCarthy and a devastating loss of someone he badly needed to protect him in the ordeal to come.

On June 11, 1954, McCarthy's nemesis, Senator Ralph E. Flanders (R. Vermont) introduced a resolution in the United States Senate to have McCarthy removed as Chair of the Senate Permanent Subcommittee on Investigations. Although there was some sentiment in Congress for McCarthy's outright dismissal, most

Senators were still too timid about the prospect of facing McCarthy's wrath and penchant for retaliation. The resolution failed.

Not one, however, to be dissuaded or intimidated, and with the President's backing, Flanders introduced Senate Resolution 301 calling for the censure of Joseph R. McCarthy.[184] The resolution contained general verbiage only, without detailed charges of wrong doing. Flanders defended its lack of specificity by arguing that the resolution targeted McCarthy's "overall pattern of behavior" rather than any particular acts or omissions. Eventually, however, the leaders of the pro-censure resolution met the same fate as Flanders' previous one. A full bill of particulars was issued listing 46 separate charges of improper conduct by McCarthy. The White House, which had been an invisible force behind the censure movement, was well pleased.

The Senate leadership appointed a special ad hoc committee to investigate the charges and report back to the full body.

The feeling was that a non-controversial, yet distinguished, member was needed to Chair the Committee. The job went to Senator Arthur V. Watkins, Republican of Utah, 47 years old, a Mormon and a former judge. A non-flamboyant and serious public servant, Watkins was tough and steadfast in a quiet, dignified way.

Watkins's first action was to bar television cameras from the hearing. Having seen the Army-McCarthy hearings, Watkins was determined not to allow the proceedings to degenerate into a public spectacle and an opportunity for the participants to substitute playing to the gallery for serious deliberation. There would be no grandstanding if Watkins could possibly prevent it. Decorum and protocol were to be observed. In particular, Watkins demanded that McCarthy conform to Senate protocol.

The first major test for Watkins came in September, 1954 when McCarthy appeared before the Watkins Committee and immediately started a verbal attack upon the Chairman. Watkins had McCarthy expelled from the room with dispatch.

---

[184] i.e. an official reprimand.

McCarthy's attack was extremely ill-advised. The United States Senate was a venerable institution and its members did not take kindly to attacks on fellow members. The incident would come back to haunt McCarthy a couple of months later.

The Senate was parsimonious in lending credence to the forty six charges. Reprimanding one of its own was put to rigorous standards. Unless a charge was proven beyond the peradventure of a doubt, censure would not be voted on that count. Little by little, the charges were whittled down.

Watkins was no less circumspect than any other committee member. When the Committee proposed to censure McCarthy for his scathing attack on General Ralph Zwicker's character and intellect, it gathered immediate support. Watkins, however, said no. General Zwicker had arguably induced McCarthy's outburst, and had to be viewed in that context. Mitigating circumstances were present, reasoned Watkins, which made the case for censure untenable. He had the Zwicker charges dropped.

As the deliberations wore on, it became clear that the Committee was not disposed to vote for censure for McCarthy's attacks on those outside the Senate.

McCarthy's anti-communist rhetoric was popular with Watkins's home base constituency in Utah. Any censure of McCarthy seemed sure to jeopardize Watkins's Senate Seat. Watkins, however, did not let personal political factors deter him from doing his job. Under his firm leadership, the tide gathered against Joe McCarthy. "His allies in the media, the House and the Senate deserted him one by one."[185]

On December 2, 1954 the Senate voted 67 to 22 to censure McCarthy. At the end of the day McCarthy's censure had been based solely upon his attacks on other members of the Senate and his disrespect to the body as a whole. On an amended resolution mentioning neither the name "Zwicker" nor the word "censure", the Senate condemned McCarthy for conduct contrary to senatorial traditions.

The President and his staff privately exulted in the Censure Resolution. They had monitored the Watkins Committee Hearings

---

[185] *History of the American People*, Id., p. 837.

— as they had the Army-McCarthy Hearings — with laser-beam intensity. The only difference was that while Eisenhower was the driving-though unseen-force behind Army-McCarthy, the same could not be said for the Censure proceedings. With its distinctive sense of tradition and independence, no one outside of the Senate Chamber could fundamentally influence the direction of the hearings. In the final analysis, the vote came down to vindicating the dignity of the Senate itself and asserting its unassailability from internal attack.

The two counts on which the Senate ultimately voted for censure were:[*]

- That McCarthy had "failed to cooperate with the Subcommittee on Rules and Administration, and had repeatedly abused the members who were trying to carry out assigned duties..."

- That McCarthy had charged three members of the Select Committee (Watkins Committee) with "deliberate deception and fraud;...that the special Senate Session was a "lynch party"; that the Committee was...the "unwitting handmaiden," "involuntary agent and attorney-in-fact" of the Communist party; and had "acted contrary to Senatorial ethics and tended to bring the Senate into dishonor and disrepute; to obstruct the constitutional processes of the Senate and to impair its dignity.

The Senate's official reprimand was worded as a vote to "condemn" McCarthy on both counts rather than "censure" him.

---

[*] See Appendix H.

The Democrats voted unanimously in favor of the Resolution and the Republican vote was equally split. Even as the echoes of the final yeas and nays faded into inaudibility, Senator H. Styles Bridges was rising to get the attention of the presiding officer. He then argued forcefully that the resolution "was not a censure resolution" since nowhere in the resolution did the word "censure" appear. His protest was successful and the word "censure" was removed from the title of Senate Resolution No. 301.

Bridges's parliamentary window dressing was far more successful within the Senate Chamber than outside. History has recorded the Senate action as a "censure" and many Senate documents refer to it that way. The media called it a "censure" from the outset and it was that word which seeped into and embedded itself in the national consciousness.

Said Senator McCarthy, "I wouldn't exactly call it a vote of confidence" but then added, "I don't feel I've been lynched."

THE WHITE HOUSE, December, 1954.

Arthur Watkins had steered the censure motion over treacherous shoals to a safe mooring. In the process McCarthy and his followers tossed verbal brick bats at Watkins at every turn. By the end of the hearings he was feeling beaten up. In the process, however, he had attained almost hero status in the eyes of the President and his lieutenants.

Late in the afternoon of December 1, 1954 White House Chief of Staff Sherman Adams told staffers that Watkins had been pushed around, had handled the job superbly and it would be nice for the President to give him sort of (a) nod of recognition.[186] There was no known consideration given by the President or White House personnel to how McCarthy would react when a man he considered a political enemy was singled out for presidential recognition.

---

[186] Memo by Ann Whitman regarding events leading up to so-called "break" by McCarthy with the White House, December 7, 1954 (DDE's Presidential Papers, Administration Series, Box 25 – McCarthy letters)

The President rejected Adams's suggestion to invite Watkins to a stag dinner scheduled for December 6, as too blatant and obvious. Even after all the time and turmoil, Ike still did not want to rub salt in McCarthy's wounds. Attorney General Brownell felt even more strongly about it, advising the President that shining such a bright spotlight on Watkins would be insensitive to the bruised feelings of those Republicans in the Senate and House who had been strenuously opposed to the censure resolution.

Finally, Eisenhower settled for simply inviting Watkins to the White House for a chat on a Saturday morning. He told James Hagerty that he wanted to see Watkins "to tell him how superbly he had handled a difficult job."[187] The President assumed his conversation with Hagerty was confidential. Hagerty reached the exact opposite conclusion — believing that what the President told him was that he wanted Hagerty "to tell the press boys after Watkins came in."[188]

Because of a rare breakdown in communications between the President and his trusted press secretary, the meeting between Watkins and the President was displayed prominently on most of the front pages of the Sunday Newspapers, including a picture of Watkins at the White House.

Predictably, McCarthy was irate. Relations between he and the President had now reached their all-time low. Ike called Hagerty into his office the first thing on Monday morning after having breakfast with Senate Majority Leader Knowland. Knowland is believed to have told the President of McCarthy's displeasure over the incident.

The President told Hagerty that he hadn't expected his remarks about Watkins to be made public. Hagerty responded that he had concluded the opposite — that the President had made the remarks for the very reason that he wanted them made public. One cannot be sure what the President's actual intentions were, but Hagerty reported to several others on the White House roster that although Ike had raised the issue, he did not really seem disturbed over the

---

[187] Id.
[188] Id.

publicity the meeting with Watkins had generated. This was not surprising.

All through the 1952 presidential campaign and the first two years of his first term, the President was consistent in his ambivalence over how to best deal with McCarthy. Ever the pragmatist, Eisenhower wanted to bring down McCarthy, but at the same time avoid a direct confrontation which would cause a schism in the Republican Party. A precedent had been established by the way he had dealt with General Montgomery during World War II. Through the use of subtlety and shrewd misdirection, Ike had frequently put the iconic British general in his place, but with a deft touch applied so as not to risk fracturing the European Alliance. This was the genius of Dwight D. Eisenhower and one of the main reasons George Marshall picked him as Commander-in-Chief to lead the allies to victory.

The Watkins incident, however, gave McCarthy the opportunity to inject drama into his fight for political survival. On December 7, 1954, he publicly announced that he was "breaking" with the Eisenhower Administration.

Ike had no public comment concerning McCarthy's "break" with him. When it happened he chose to ignore it. But more than a decade later, he seemed compelled to tie up the loose ends of his life, in his memoirs. In "Mandate for Change, 1953-1956," he included the following passages as a kind of historical postscript to the entire McCarthy era. Seldom before or after did Dwight D. Eisenhower write with such conviction and emotion:

"Upon learning of this meeting" (i.e. December 4, 1954 White House meeting between Senator Watkins and President Eisenhower), "Senator McCarthy, finally made what has been termed his 'break' with me — why it was called such at that late date I could not fathom. He claimed that the administration was soft on communism and apologized for having supported me in 1952."[189]

"But one thing was apparent. By a combination of the vote and the loss of his committee chairmanship, the Senator's power was ended. Senator McCarthy died an untimely and sad — even pathetic

---

[189] Mandate for Change, Id., p. 330.

— death in 1957, but as a political force he was finished at the end of 1954."

Senator Joseph R. McCarthy had overplayed his hand — first in the Army-McCarthy hearings — followed in swift sequence in the Senate Censure Hearings.

One's inspiration of choice in literature for McCarthy could well be Julius Caesar; but with no loss in the power of imagery, it could just as easily have been Brutus; for McCarthy was betrayed, but — mainly by himself.

CHAPTER ELEVEN

Aftermath

After December 2, 1954, Joseph R. McCarthy was in free fall. He began to drink more heavily than ever. Back in June 1950, Senator Margaret Chase Smith of Maine had the moxey to speak out against McCarthy's caucuses with his Senate allies, calling them "a rendezvous for vilification" Hers was a lonely voice, however, in 1950. But McCarthy's allies in Congress and the media had deserted him in droves by December, 1954.

After the censure vote McCarthy soldiered on in the Senate for another two and a half years. But Congress had become his "House of Usher," strewn with the ruins and remnants of a shattered career, which once had been so promising.

Colleagues walked out of their way to avoid him. His speeches in the Senate were delivered to a mainly empty chamber in which sad echoes of his sonorous voice seemed laden with rebuke. Most of those not abandoning the cavernous room out-did themselves in conspicuous displays of indifference and inattention.

The work-a-day beat reporters, columnists and editors of the D.C. Press Corps — untethered as they were to him by collegial ties — now ignored him completely; whereas at the height of his power and influence they had hung on his every utterance. His outside speaking engagements shrank to almost nothing — his banishment was nearly total.

After the censure, colleagues observed McCarthy to be in a state of physical and emotional decline. The ravages of alcoholism were making him old, well before his time. He was only forty five at the time of the censure vote and a political come-back was not beyond the realm of possibility. But McCarthy was a burned out case. Despite that, he was still feisty in public as he steadfastly decried communism in America. Friends told him he was drinking far too much but their well-meaning warnings were met with defiance. When his old friend, Urban Van Susteren, said "You're killing yourself, god dammit," McCarthy retorted with, "Kiss my ass, Van."[190]

He warned against attendance at summit conferences with Communist world leaders, saying "you cannot offer friendship to tyrants and murderers...without advancing the cause of tyranny and murder....that co-existence with communists is neither possible nor honorable nor desirable. Our long term objective must be the eradication of Communism from the face of the earth."[191] To further this end, Senator McCarthy introduced Senate Resolution 116 on June 20, 1955,* which sought to compel the discussion of freeing Communist and Communist bloc countries of all major international conferences.

Although McCarthy sustained many self-inflicted wounds during the halcyon years of his career — from 1950 through 1954 — many influential persons also played a direct role in bringing him down. Margaret Chase Smith, Ralph Flanders, Anthony V. Watkins, Edward R. Murrow, Stuart Symington, William Benton, Joseph Welch and Dwight D. Eisenhower were among his most effective adversaries. But none was more instrumental in his decline and fall than Eisenhower.

Although declaring to his advisers on more than one occasion that, "I will not get down in the gutter with that guy," Ike

---

[190] The Fifties, Id., p. 252.
[191] The New Isolationism, A Study of Politics and Foreign Policy since 1950, Norman A. Graebner (Ronald Press, 1956) p. 227.
* Senate Resolution 116: (See Exhibit G.)

assiduously warred against McCarthy out of view of the public eye. When a White House official described a new kind of life insurance, a sudden-death policy you could take out on someone else, Eisenhower observed grimly, "I know one fellow I'd like to take that policy out for."[192] And as McCarthy's popularity waned, Ike quipped to his staff, "There is no longer McCarthyism. It is now McCarthywasim."[193]

McCarthy remained combative even after his "break" with the President in December of 1954.

He fought Eisenhower to the very end. Though described by his biographer, Fred J. Cook, as a "pale-ghost of his former self,"[194] he summoned up the energy to oppose President Eisenhower's nomination of William J. Brennan to the United States Supreme Court, after reading a speech by Brennan in which he called McCarthy's anti-communist investigations "witch hunts." Perhaps a metaphor for his painful isolation was the fact that Senator McCarthy was the only Senator to vote against Brennan's nomination.

If we were to look at the Ike-McCarthy saga simply in terms of winners and losers, Eisenhower clearly won by a knock-out. The President's skill, deviousness and shrewdness ensured the survival of the Country and its democratic institutions. As a result, wrote historian Paul Johnson, the nation emerged — without too much damage — from one of its periodic outbreaks of hysteria, which in this case goes under the heading of McCarthyism."[195]

Johnson's fellow historian, Richard Hofstadter, described the phenomenon, McCarthyism, "as a projection onto society of the groundless fears of pseudo-conservatives." The title alone of Hofstadter's 1964 essay, "The Paranoid Style in American Politics" suggested a mass pathology.

While a case can certainly be made that the pejoratives used by Johnson and Hofstadter: "hysteria," "groundless fears" and

---

[192] The Fifties, Id., p. 252.
[193] Enemies Within: Joe McCarthy, The Smithsonian Channel, 12/26/12.
[194] The Nightmare Decade, the Life and Times of Senator Joe McCarthy, Fred J. Cook (Random House, 1971), p. 537.
[195] The History of the American People Id., p. 833.

"paranoia", may have provided some convenient labels to paste on McCarthyism in substitution for real historical analysis. However, they provide little insight into McCarthyism's historical and anthropological significance, which were profound.

It wasn't Joseph McCarthy himself that made the early 1950s such an unsettling era of American history. He was simply one very flawed man and there was little about him which was special or distinctive. He wasn't even the biggest demagogue to traipse across America's political stage. Yes, McCarthy suffered a precipitous decline and a personally tragic fall from grace. But it might have been little noticed and faded into obscurity, had it not been for the greater plunge of the American people from 1950 through 1954 into a river of moral cowardice.

In his masterpiece, "The Fifties," David Halberstam wrote that during the Army-McCarthy hearings, "McCarthy had done himself in with ugliness." Implied in that declaration is the message that McCarthy's contumacious abuse of people's most fundamental civil liberties, his malicious destruction of careers and reputations and his intentional alienation of citizen from citizen, neighbor from neighbor and ideology from ideology, during the five years preceding the Army-McCarthy hearings, was not enough to cause his downfall. The American people had in fact helped him survive all of that until he came across as mean, rude and otherwise unattractive on television. When that happened, the bubble burst and the image was shattered beyond repair.

The adjectives used in the Senate resolution censuring McCarthy's conduct included, "contemptuous, contumacious, denunciatory, unworthy, inexcusable and reprehensible." But until McCarthy imploded in the Spring of 1954, hardly a single American had the moral courage to publicly apply such strong words to his behavior.

Permissiveness of McCarthy's deplorable tactics was practically universal. It started at the top — in the White House — and gravitated down from there. As instrumental as he was in ultimately bringing McCarthy down, President Eisenhower never repudiated McCarthy or McCarthyism publicly. In fact, he is not known to have ever spoken McCarthy's name publicly during his presidency. Yet it was Eisenhower who engineered the Army-McCarthy hearings — in order to expose McCarthy's misdeeds to the public.

Eisenhower's defense of his posture toward McCarthy finally came in his memoirs, Mandate for Change, 1952 to 1956, which were published in 1964. There statements appeared which exposed an ambivalence on Eisenhower's part as to the best way to handle McCarthy.

At page 330, Eisenhower wrote: "I did have an urge to go back into my memory to review the developments and to contemplate their meaning. McCarthyism took its toll on many individuals and on the nation. No one was safe from charges recklessly made from inside the walls of congress..."

Yet while deploring the "mental anguish unfairly inflicted upon people" (page 331), Ike chose to defend his practice of public silence about McCarthy more in terms reflecting broad concepts of jurisprudence and political philosophy than an immediate threat to the welfare of the nation and its citizens:

> "McCarthyism was a much larger issue than McCarthy. This was the truth that I constantly held before me as I listened to the many exhortations that I should 'demolish' the Senator himself. Although he was striving to make himself the embodiment of the anti-communist, anti-subversive movement in the United States, he too often forgot the complex and precious American issues of personal liberties and constitutional process...His avowed purpose became hopelessly entangled with and frustrated by his methods. It was his methods that were labeled as McCarthyism...Lashing back at one man, which is easy enough for a President, was not as important to me as the long-term value of restraint, the due process of law and the basic rights of free men." (Mandate for Change, 1952 to 1956, p. 321).

Should the President of the United States, whose functions included the faithful execution of the laws in order to secure the general welfare, have exercised less restraint? Should he have been more proactive in exposing McCarthy and combating his actions? Would the lives and reputations of many innocent Americans have been protected had Eisenhower chosen to forcefully and openly oppose McCarthyism. These are propositions about which reasonable men can, and do, differ.

In writing about the Senate's censure of McCarthy at page 330 of <u>Mandate for Change</u>, Eisenhower rightfully took some of the credit for the success of the censure resolution:

> "It is doubtful that the result (i.e. censure) would ever have come about had I adopted the habit of referring to McCarthy by name in press conferences..."

But the question still remains. Was the censure resolution more important than — to use Eisenhower's word — "demolishing" McCarthy sooner and thereby preventing him from doing so much additional human damage? One doubts that a satisfactory answer to this question can be given without having experienced first-hand the temper of the times. One thing does seem clear. For a national leader to have taken on McCarthy directly and publicly during the first four years of the 1950's would have taken tremendous moral courage — the type of courage demonstrated by Lincoln on the issues of slavery and preservation of the Union in 1861; or perhaps by Truman in firing the iconic General Douglas McArthur in 1951 at the height of the Korean War. Maybe it's just this kind of courage that separates a great president from a merely good president. But any credible judgment must factor in that Eisenhower's patient approach did ultimately work. And there is no way of knowing whether a more confrontational approach would have been effective. Was wisdom here the better part of valor?

The temper of the times, however, did not just include the Red scare and the Cold War. It also included the fact that the United States was being led by a national hero of monumental proportions. The nagging feeling that he could have done more remains.

Moving down the scale from the White House to the Congress, to the news media and to the public also points to a national failure of moral courage over McCarthyism.

Joseph McCarthy was not a sophisticated politician. He was not sly or crafty by nature. Rarely had he been accused of being two-faced. With McCarthy what you saw was pretty much what you got. From the beginning to end of his ascendancy and decline — he stayed in character — seldom employing subtlety in place of overt insult; antagonizing colleagues and those above him on the Washington power grid, with equal relish. His alcoholism appeared to dull his survival instincts and contribute to his recklessness.

For almost five years, however, McCarthy's fellow members of Congress either appeased him or aggressively participated in his activities and avowed dogma. The U.S. Senate, the body which gave birth to his movement and nurtured its development, only turned against him after his popularity had plummeted and he had become a public embarrassment. But even after Senator William Benton had introduced his censure resolution, the body showed great reluctance to deal substantially with McCarthy's civil liberties violations, slander and demagoguery. In the end the censure resolution had been scaled back to include only instances of abuse and hostility to his fellow Senators and to Senate Committees. Even the count of Resolution S. 301 which chastised McCarthy for his extreme personal attack on General Ralph Zwicker was dropped on the eve of the final vote. And nowhere did the term "McCarthyism" appear in the resolution. The straw which broke the camel's back had nothing to do with his anti-communist crusade against various individuals and their organizations. Rather, it occurred when he accused the select committee studying the censure charges and its conservative Republican chairman, Arthur V. Watkins, of being an "unwitting handmaiden of the Communist Party."

As late as January of 1954, Joe McCarthy was still very popular with a sizeable majority of the American people. It's not as though the public was kept in the dark about the excesses of McCarthyism. Everything McCarthy said or did was big news — much of it captured in screaming headlines. But it seemed as though the collective conscience of America had been asleep since February of

1950. It took television — particularly the broadcasts of Edward R. Murrow and the Army-McCarthy Hearings — to shake them out of their moral lassitude. The mass stupor ended dramatically and permanently when Joseph Welch spoke the words, "At long last, Sir, have you no decency?" on June 9, 1954. Welch delivered his famous coup de grace to McCarthy but it also smashed once and for all the paranoia of the public which was the underpinning of McCarthyism.

Edward R. Murrow's trenchant observations on the news medias' complicity in the flowering of McCarthyism came years later when he summed up McCarthy as "a politically unsophisticated man with a flair for publicity, whose weapon was fear."[196] Murrow went on to elaborate:

> [He was] in a real sense the creature of the mass media. They made him. They gave nationwide circulation to his mouthings. They defended their actions on the grounds that what he said was news, when they knew he lied....He polluted the channels of communication, and every radio and television network, every newspaper and magazine publisher who did not speak out against him, contributed to his evil work and must share part of the responsibility for what he did, not only to our fellow citizens but to our self-respect....
>
> It has been said repeatedly that television caused his downfall. This is not precisely true. His prolonged exposure during the so-called Army-McCarthy hearings certainly did something to diminish his stature. He became something of a bore. But his downfall really stemmed from the fact that he broke the rules of the club, the United States Senate. When he began attacking the integrity the loyalty of

---

[196] _Murrow_, Id., p. 471.

fellow Senators, he was censured by that body, and was finished.[197]

After his censure, McCarthy also was stripped of the chairmanship of the Investigations Subcommittee of the Committee on Governmental Operations.

In 1956, he gave a rare televised interview in which he was asked pointedly whether he believed President Eisenhower was under the influence of the communists. McCarthy was still enough of a politician to avoid accusing the President directly. He stayed in character, however, by answering that although the President wasn't under communist influence, the men around him were. When the interviewer asked him to name names, McCarthy named Dr. Milton Eisenhower, Sherman Adams and C.D. Jackson. He paused and seemed about to name others when he stated, "Let's just leave it at that."[198]

Joe McCarthy did enjoy some domestic happiness during the last couple of years of his life after he and his wife, the former Jean Kerr, adopted a baby girl. But even this was tainted by McCarthy's excessive drinking. Told by his doctors that he had to give up alcohol completely or it would kill him, McCarthy drank anyway and "in effect, committed suicide."[199] McCarthy reportedly suffered from cirrhosis of the liver and during the last couple of years was frequently hospitalized for alcoholism. Journalist Richard Rovere in 1959 wrote of McCarthy's addiction:

> He had always been a heavy drinker, and there were times in those seasons of discontent when he drank more than ever. But he was not always drunk. He went on the wagon (for him this meant beer instead of whiskey) for days and weeks at a time. The difficulty toward the end was that he couldn't hold the stuff. He

[197] EPM, "Television and Politics", Guildhall London, October 19, 1959.
[198] Enemies Within: Joe McCarthy. The Smithsonian Channel, 12/26/12.
[199] Id.

went to pieces on his second or third drink. And he did not snap back quickly.[200]

Eyewitnesses, including Senate Aide George Reedy and journalist Tom Wicker, provided accounts of seeing McCarthy alarmingly intoxicated in the Senate while it was in session.

Senator Joseph R. McCarthy died on May 2, 1957 in Bethesda Naval Hospital. He was 48. The official cause of death listed on his death certificate was acute hepatitis, an inflammation of the liver. The consensus among his biographers, however, is that he died of alcoholism. More than thirty thousand filed through St. Mary's Church in Appleton, Wisconsin to pay their last respects. Joseph McCarthy remained a hero in the eyes of many in his native state of Wisconsin.

Dwight David Eisenhower served two distinguished terms as President of the United States and is today revered as one of America's greatest heroes. He died on March 28, 1969 at the age of 78. He is not known to ever have mentioned Joseph McCarthy's name publicly except in his memoirs, "Mandate for Change".

[200] Senator Joe McCarthy by Richard Rovere, U. of Calif Press, 1959.

BIBLIOGRAPHY

The Fifties by David Halberstam (Villard Books, 1953)

The Guns of Last Light by Rick Atkinson (Henry Holt & Co., LLC, 2013)

Ike's Bluff by Evan Thomas (Little Brown and Co., 2012)

Murrow, His Life & times by A. M. Sperber (Freundlick Books, 1987)

Mandate For Change, 1953-1956 by Dwight D. Eisenhower (Doubleday, 1963)

Eisenhower & the Anti-Communist Crusade by Jeff Broadwater (University of North Carolina Press, 1992)

The Nightmare Decade : The Life & Times of Joe McCarthy by Fred J. Cook (Random House, 1971)

Harry & Ike by Steve Neal (Scribner, 2001)

U.S. News & World Report (September, 1952)

The Presidential Papers of Dwight David Eisenhower, the Eisenhower Presidential Library and Museum

The Presidency of Dwight David Eisenhower (Wikipedia.org)

Presidential Politics, Eisenhower, WGBH The American Experience (PBS)

Enemies Within : Joe McCarthy (The Smithsonian Channel, 12/26/12)

Truman by David McCullough (Touchstone, 1992)

The History of the American People, Vol. II, by Paul Johnson (Easton Press, 1997)

Alger Hiss, Why He Chose Treason, by Cristina Shelton (Threshold Editions, 2012)

The New Dealers War: FDR and the War Within WWII by Thomas Fleming (Basic Books, 2001)

Nightmare in Red: The McCarthy Era in Perspective by Richard M. Fried (Oxford University Press)

McCarthyism, The Great American Scare: A Documentary History by Albert Fried (Oxford University Press, 1997)

The C.D. Jackson Papers, 1953, The Dwight D. Eisenhower Presidential Library and Museum

Voice of America, A History by Alan L. Heil (Columbia University Press, 2003)

The Politics of Fear: Joseph R. McCarthy & The Senate by Robert Griffith (University of Massachusetts Press)

Ike, An American Hero by Michael Korda (Harper, 2007)

The James C. Haggerty Papers, 1954, The Dwight D. Eisenhower Library and Museum

The Congressional Record, March 9, 1954

The Museum of Broadcast Communications (www.museum.tv/archives.McCarthy/Army)

Joseph McCarthy, (Wikipedia.org)

NBC Nightly News, Tom Brokaw and Peter Williams, 5/5/03 (NBS Universal Media, LLC)

Edward R. Murrow With the News (CBS News, 5/28/54)

Point of Order, Emile D. Antonio (Documentary Film, 1964)

Anatomy of a Counter-Bar Association, The Chicago Counsel of Lawyers by Michael Powell (28 July 2006)

The Army-McCarthy Hearings, 1954 by Robert D. Marcus and Anthony Marcus (Brandywine Press, 1998)

Not Without Honor: The History of Anti-Communism by Richard Gid Powers (Yale University Press, 1998)

The New Isolationism, A Study of Politics and Foreign Policy Since 1950 by Norman A. Graebner (Ronald Press, 1956)

FPM, Television & Politics", Guildhall Loudon, October 19, 1959

Senator Joe McCarthy by Richard Rovere (University of California Press, 1959)

Adlai Stevenson, His Life & Legacy by Porter McKeever (Quill, William Morrow New York, 1989)

Harry S. Truman by Margaret Truman (William Morrow & Company, Inc., New York, 1973)

Partners in Command, George Marshall and Dwight Eisenhower in War and Peace, by Mark Perry (The Penguin Press, 2007)

How McCarthyism Worked by Alia Holt (History.howstuffworks.com)

*Hungerford Cy, artist. "**An Uncomfortable Situation**." December 3, 1953.
Prints and Photographs Division, Library of Congress*

Sixth Draft - Communism and Freedom

To defend freedom, in short, is -- first of all -- to respect freedom. That respect demands another, quite simple kind of respect -- respect for the integrity of fellow citizens who enjoy their right to disagree. The right to question a man's judgment carries with it no automatic right to question his honor.

With respect to one case I shall be quite specific. I know that charges of disloyalty have in the past been levelled against General George C. Marshall. Any of his alleged errors in judgment while serving in capacities other than military, I am not here discussing. But I was privileged throughout the years of World War II to know General Marshall personally, as Chief of Staff of the Army. I know him, as a man and a soldier, to be dedicated with singular selflessness and the profoundest patriotism to the service of America. Here we have a sobering lesson of the way freedom must not defend itself.

Armed with this clear and uncompromising respect for freedom, how then shall we defend it?

JOHN L. McCLELLAN, ARK., CHAIRMAN
CLYDE R. HOEY, N. C.   JOSEPH R. McCARTHY, WIS.
HERBERT R. O'CONOR, MD.   KARL E. MUNDT, S. DAK.
HUBERT H. HUMPHREY, MINN.   MARGARET CHASE SMITH, MAINE
MIKE MONRONEY, OKLA.   ANDREW F. SCHOEPPEL, KANS.
THOMAS R. UNDERWOOD, KY.   HENRY C. DWORSHAK, IDAHO
BLAIR MOODY, MICH.   RICHARD M. NIXON, CALIF.

WALTER L. REYNOLDS, CHIEF CLERK

United States Senate

COMMITTEE ON
GOVERNMENT OPERATIONS

February 3, 1953

The President
The White House

Dear Mr. President:

I understand that the matter of the confirmation of James B. Conant as High Commissioner in Germany will come before the Senate within the next few days. I feel as a courtesy to you, that I should inform you of the position which I shall take when this matter comes to the Senate floor.

I am strongly opposed to Mr. Conant's confirmation on the following four principal grounds:

1. His speech made in New York City on October 7, 1944, which, in my opinion, can be interpreted only as advocating the destruction of all industry in Western Germany, as shortly thereafter advocated in the Morgenthau Plan, which, as you know, was to a great extent prepared by Harry Dexter White. I feel that the Morgenthau Plan was completely unrealistic and played directly into the hands of our enemy. In fact, I believe Mr. Cordell Hull referred to it as a plan of "blind vengeance" and that you referred to the plan as "silly and tragic". You understand, of course, that I am not taking the position that Mr. Conant collaborated with Morgenthau or Harry Dexter White, but his plan covered in his speech was the same in its essential aspect, namely the destruction of industry in Western Germany.

2. His article in May of 1940 in the *Atlantic Monthly*, entitled "Education for Classless Society". Therein he states:

   "If the American ideal is not to be an illusion the citizens of this republic must not shrink from drastic action. The requirement, however, is not a radical expropriation of wealth at any given moment, it is rather a continuous process by which power and privilege may be automatically redistributed at the end of each generation."

It will be noted here that he opposes the Communist idea of a "radical expropriation of wealth at any given moment", but that he does favor a process by which the wealth will be automatically distributed at the end of each generation.

-2-

The President

This can mean only one thing, namely one hundred percent inheritance tax, which, of course, would ultimately result in the complete socialization of any country.

3. His opposition to parochial schools. He obviously has a right to oppose parochial schools and is undoubtedly honest in his opposition. However, as you know, most of the Germans are either Catholic or Lutheran and the parochial school subject is one upon which they feel very strongly. It would, therefore, seem that to appoint a man as High Commissioner of Germany who opposes the type of school system which is the heart of the educational system of Germany and about which those people feel so strongly will create a great deal of ill feeling toward America and furnish ammunition for the Communist propaganda guns.

4. His recent speech in which he first states that if there are Communists in colleges they should be rooted out by the Government, but then states that if an investigation were made and a few Communists found, the damage done would be greater than the harm in their remaining as educators. At the same time, you will recall, he stated there are no Communists at Harvard. It may be that Harlow Shapley, Kirtley Mather, and the late F. O. Matthiessen are not and were not Communists, but the surprise would lie in finding that out. They have been up early every morning doing the work of the Communist Party; they have espoused Communist causes on occasion after occasion. The reasonable presumption is that if they teach at Harvard they are intelligent men. If they are intelligent men and work sedulously in behalf of Communist causes, then the most reasonable inference is that they are doing so because they are either Communist or pro-Communist. They apparently are so recognized by everyone except Mr. Conant.

Let me make it clear that I do not accuse Mr. Conant of being either Communist or pro-Communist. However, I strongly feel that his innocent statements about Communist activities in education and about the presence of communism in his own faculty indicate a woeful lack of knowledge of the vicious and intricate Communist conspiracy. Certainly it doesn't show any qualifications for the task of safeguarding the American Embassy at Bonn against Communist penetration, nor with the task of meeting the Communist threat in Western Germany.

Let me make it clear that I feel that undoubtedly Mr. Conant is a fine gentleman. He also is apparently intelligent -- intelligent enough to have said on one occasion when addressing a Convocation of the University of New York in 1947, that he was greatly concerned by the fact that many temperamentally unsuited persons were making their way into universities.

-3-

The President

And he added: After all, "I can imagine a native scientist or
philosopher, with strong loyalties to the advancement of civilization,
and the unity of the world, who would be a questionable asset to a
government department charged with negotiations with another nation.
The same men, on the other hand, because of their professional com-
petence, might make excellent professors."

Feeling as strongly as I do that Mr. Conant is not qualified for
the job in Germany, normally I would put up an all-out fight on the
Senate floor in an attempt to prevent his confirmation. I frankly
would do that now if I thought there were any possibility of defeating
him. However, I am convinced that many Senators who might normally
question Conant's fitness will go along with the new President, who
has received such an overwhelming vote of confidence from the American
people.

This presents a very serious question of what would be gained or lost
for this country and the peace of the world by greatly publicizing what
I consider Mr. Conant's shortcomings for this job. I greatly fear that
an all-out fight on my part against Conant, which I normally would feel
compelled to make, would not accomplish his defeat and would furnish
the Communists in Europe a vast amount of ammunition for their guns.
For that reason, I have very reluctantly decided that while I shall
vote against Mr. Conant, I shall not make any public statements in
regard to him at this time, nor is this letter being made public by
me. I might add that this is one of the most difficult decisions I
have ever made. I feel that whichever course I take damage is being
done. I am choosing what I consider the lesser of the two evils.

Wishing you good luck and good health, I remain

                                        Very sincerely yours,

                                        JOE McCARTHY

McC:db

May 18, 1953.

Personal and Confidential

Dear Harry:

I emphatically agree with most of what you have to say in
your letter of May ninth. I shall certainly take seriously
your observation about the Judd case.

With respect to McCarthy, I continue to believe that the
President of the United States cannot afford to name names
in opposing procedures, practices and methods in our government. This applies with special force when the individual
concerned enjoys the immunity of a United States Senator.
This particular individual wants, above all else, publicity.
Nothing would probably please him more than to get the
publicity that would be generated by public repudiation by
the President.

I do not mean that there is no possibility that I shall ever
change my mind on this point. I merely mean that as of
this moment, I consider that the wisest course of action
is to continue to pursue a steady, positive policy in foreign
relations, in legal procedures in cleaning out the insecure
and the disloyal, and in all other areas where McCarthy seems
to take such a specific and personal interest. My friends on
the Hill tell me that of course, among other things, he wants
to increase his appeal as an after-dinner speaker and so raise
the fees that he charges.

Personal and Confidential

Personal and Confidential

Mr. Bullis - 2.

It is a sorry mess; at times one feels almost like hanging his head in shame when he reads some of the unreasoned, vicious outbursts of demagoguery that appear in our public prints. But whether a Presidential "crack down" would better, or would actually worsen, the situation, is a moot question.

With all the best,

As ever,

x PP+ 27.5

Mr. Harry Bullis,
General Mills Incorporated,
400 Second Avenue South,
Minneapolis 1, Minnesota.

Personal and Confidential

MEMORANDUM OF DECEMBER 1, 1953

TO: MR. MURRAY SNYDER

FROM: STANLEY M. RUMBOUGH, JR. and CHARLES MASTERSON

SUBJECT: RESPONDING TO SENATOR McCARTHY

XW.C.

XPPF 1-CC

I.   MAIN POINTS FOR CONSIDERATION

A. Senator McCarthy has attacked the President, and the President's prestige is threatened both in this country and abroad.

B. Would a response by the President lend dignity and status to the attack?

C. Will a response to McCarthy jeopradize the legislative program?

II. SUPPLEMENTARY FACTS

A. Image of the President as an inspirational leader is important to the independent voter, who provided the margin of victory in the last election. These men and women did not vote for the Republican Party; they voted for Eisenhower. If their image of the President becomes clouded and if they do not vote again as they did in the last election, no amount of effort by the Republican Party will bring success.

B. The threat to the legislative program is highly questionable. There are qualified observers who say that McCarthy and his coterie will neither drag their feet nor vote with the Democrats in the event the President speaks out against McCarthyism. Furthermore, there is no assurance that appeasement now will insure the legislative program. It is apparent that Senator McCarthy acts exclusively in the interest of Senator McCarthy, and if he deems it good strategy to discredit Eisenhower by scuttling the legislative program he will do so, whether or not the President speaks out against McCarthyism.

C. People are swayed by emotion more than by reason. And this is an emotional issue. Furthermore, the image of the President as a fighter may well be more important politically than the success or failure of a legislative program, (assuming that success or failure of the program is involved.).

D. One of the most dramatic moments in the President's career has arrived. He can appeal to the people now as a popular

PAGE TWO
MEMORANDUM

leader who has been attacked. Further, in speaking out against
McCarthyism he is on the side of the angels. He can answer
McCarthyism in the spirit of fair play and in the very words of
the founding fathers, the Bill of Rights, Washington and Lincoln.

III. SUGGESTED ACTION

A. Televise the press conference - on Thursday instead
of Wednesday to allow more time for a build-up. This is a dramatic
moment for the first televised press conference and can be explained
partly on the basis of the N.Y. newspaper strike and partly on the
need to match the coverage McCarthy had when he issued his challenge.

B. Get Secretary Dulles to answer specific McCarthy
charges re Davies, American flyers in Korea, and trade with Communists.

C. Start off the press conference with a statement including such concepts as:

This Administration is determined to keep the people
informed. We have been charged on the one hand with harboring
Communists and on the other hand with playing politics in our program
of cleaning Communists out. The record of this Administration is
open to public view - and it is a record we are and will be proud of.

As I have stated before, the era in which we live is
dominated by the threat of world domination by the forces of Communism. If our way of life is to be preserved, we must be alert to
that threat. Blindness or poor judgment in detecting Communist influence in our government is as dangerous as excesses in the other
direction.

Speaking for that part of the Administration that is
my responsibility, I can say that we shall not be guided by political
motives in our fight against the Communist threat and we shall not
be cajoled or challenged into abandoning the traditional American
spriit of fair play. We shall be vigilant but not fanatical.

May 17, 1954

Dear Mr. Secretary:

It has long been recognized that to assist the Congress in
achieving its legislative purposes every Executive Department
or Agency must, upon the request of a Congressional
Committee, expeditiously furnish information relating to
any matter within the jurisdiction of the Committee, with
certain historical exceptions -- some of which are pointed
out in the attached memorandum from the Attorney General.
This Administration has been and will continue to be diligent
in following this principle.   However, it is essential to the
successful working of our system that the persons entrusted
with power in any one of the three great branches of Government shall not encroach upon the authority confided to the
others.   The ultimate responsibility for the conduct of the
Executive Branch rests with the President.

Within this Constitutional framework each branch should
cooperate fully with each other for the common good.   However, throughout our history the President has withheld
information whenever he found that what was sought was
confidential or its disclosure would be incompatible with the
public interest or jeopardize the safety of the Nation.

Because it is essential to efficient and effective administration that employees of the Executive Branch be in a position
to be completely candid in advising with each other on official
matters, and because it is not in the public interest that any
of their conversations or communications, or any documents
or reproductions, concerning such advice be disclosed, you
will instruct employees of your Department that in all of their
appearances before the Subcommittee of the Senate Committee
on Operations regarding the inquiry now before it, they are
not to testify to any such conversations or communications or
to produce any such documents or reproductions.   This principle must be maintained regardless of who would be benefited
by such disclosures.

I direct this action so as to maintain the proper separation
of powers between the Executive and Legislative Branches of
the Government in accordance with my responsibilities and
duties under the Constitution. This separation is vital to
preclude the exercise of arbitrary power by any branch of
the Government.

By this action I am not in any way restricting the testimony
of such witnesses as to what occurred regarding any matters
where the communication was directly between any of the
principals in the controversy within the Executive Branch on
the one hand and a member of the Subcommittee or its staff
on the other.

Sincerely,

The Honorable
The Secretary of Defense
Washington, D. C.

(By Hand)

www.ingramcontent.com/pod-product-compliance
Lightning Source LLC
Chambersburg PA
CBHW030012290326
41934CB00005B/313